Ira Neimark, Carla Fendi, and Aldo Pinto at Bergdorf Goodman's reopening party following 1983 renovations. (Photo courtesy of Women's Wear Daily.*)*

THE RISE *of* FASHION
and Lessons Learned
at Bergdorf Goodman

Ira Neimark

FAIRCHILD BOOKS · NEW YORK

Executive Editor: OLGA T. KONTZIAS
Assistant Acquisitions Editor: AMANDA BRECCIA
Development Editor: ROB PHELPS
Assistant Art Director: SARAH SILBERG
Production Director: GINGER HILLMAN
Production Editor: ANDREW FARGNOLI
Assistant Production Editor: LAUREN VLASSENKO
Copyeditor: JOANNE SLIKE
Ancillaries Editor: NOAH SCHWARTZBERG
Executive Director & General Manager: MICHAEL SCHLUTER
Associate Director of Sales: MELANIE SANKEL
Junior Account Manager: ALYSON SOBOTI
Cover and Text Design: CAROLYN ECKERT
Cover Art: ILLUSTRATION PROVIDED BY ANN R. COHEN
Page Layout: TOM HELLEBERG

Library of Congress Catalog Card Number: 2011920743

ISBN: 978-1-60901-318-9

GST R 133004424

Printed in the United States of America

TP09

For my wonderful grandchildren,

Russell, Hallie, Pamela, Mallory, and Elizabeth, who,

with their enthusiasm for my first book,

Crossing Fifth Avenue to Bergdorf Goodman,

encouraged me to continue to share the many stories

about my career in the world of fashion.

CONTENTS

Extraordinary Times

Experiences Learned along the Way

PREFACE

L ITTLE DID I REALIZE when I wrote my first book, *Crossing Fifth Avenue to Bergdorf Goodman*, that the book would take on a life of its own. Through the book I met many wonderful people who introduced me to the world of lecturing at business schools such as Columbia University, New York University, The Wharton School of the University of Pennsylvania, and Fashion Institute of Technology, as well as business groups from around the world.

Through the guidance of Gregg Furman, the CEO of the Luxury Marketing Council, and Robert Reiss, host of *The CEO Show*, I met students and businesspeople, all asking the same question:

Was there a secret to my success in building Bergdorf Goodman to become the leading luxury fashion store in not only New York City but also the entire United States with a fashion reputation known throughout the capitals of the world?

Possibly. If there was a secret, it was my being a survivor. I began my retail career during the Great Depression, worked my way up the ladder, and had the great good fortune to associate with some of the best retailers here in this country, as well as abroad.

With their questions and tremendous interest in all that I have been learning over these many years, I realized that I could graphically show the history and progress of Bergdorf Goodman and the growth of fashion retailing as I experienced it. It is my hope that *The Rise of Fashion and Lessons Learned at Bergdorf*

Ira Neimark. (Photo by Thomas Iannaccone courtesy of Women's Wear Daily.*)*

Goodman will inspire others, particularly students, to realize that opportunity is there for everyone, as it once was for me.

    The Rise of Fashion and Lessons Learned at Bergdorf Goodman is a companion book to *Crossing Fifth Avenue to Bergdorf Goodman*. The memoir *Crossing Fifth Avenue* covers the full span of my career, from my Horatio Alger–like introduction into the world of retailing, through my education in New England into the business of retailing, and into the initial steps I took to bring

Bergdorf Goodman to become the leading fashion specialty store. *The Rise of Fashion* focuses primarily on what was done to bring Bergdorf Goodman to its fashion leadership position, but also on how and why Bergdorf helped build the fashion industry during this period. Equally important, this book concludes with my views on how many retailers today have taken steps to increase their profits by reducing the expense of experienced salespeople, resulting in the loss of sales and customer loyalty. Finally, throughout the book I have threaded "Lessons Learned," developed through trial and error over many successful years; my ambition in writing this book is to share these lessons with younger generations who aspire to succeed in the business of luxury fashion or any other career.

ACKNOWLEDGMENTS

WITH THE COMPLETION of *The Rise of Fashion and Lessons Learned at Bergdorf Goodman*, I want to thank all those who helped me. This effort has allowed me to write and to record not only what happened to me, from the late thirties up to the early nineties, but also the history of the luxury fashion business during that time.

Throughout the book there are many, many photos and news articles. Most are from *Women's Wear Daily*, to whom I owe a debt of gratitude.

I would like to thank Edward Nardoza, editor in chief of *Women's Wear Daily,* in particular, who once again encouraged me and helped make all of the valuable material in the book available to me. Thanks also, to David Moin, senior editor, for his wise guidance and input.

I must thank Ed Nardoza again, who, after reading the first draft of *The Rise of Fashion*, asked me to show the manuscript to Beth Tighe, former general manager of Fairchild Books, who liked the manuscript enough to introduce me to Olga Kontzias, executive editor at Fairchild. Olga then put *The Rise of Fashion* into high gear by assigning Rob Phelps, the development editor, to take charge of the manuscript. I would be remiss without special thanks to Molly Monosky, Fairchild's archivist, who was always available when I was searching for photographs that only she could find. Molly's additional photos take the book to another level. Assistant art director Sarah Silverberg added the final touches.

My thanks to Arthur Sulzberger Jr., chairman and publisher of *The New York Times*, who directed me to Phyllis Callazo, of *The New York Times* photos archives. In addition to her help, my old friend Bill Cunningham generously added many photos of what went on during the most interesting time for growth of luxury fashion to the book.

Thanks to Laura Harris. With her help, I was able to obtain the photos from the *New York Post* of Eugenia Sheppard's French couture designer's party at Maxim's in Paris.

To Chris Alimena, who took me through the labyrinth of my computer. His professionalism and knowledge enabled me to produce this book.

My thanks, again, to my literary agent, Maryann Karinch of The Rudy Agency, whose constant good-natured prodding and advice made the book possible. My many, many thanks and grateful appreciation to my good friend and counsel Jeffry Aronsson. Always there with the wisdom of Solomon. My appreciation to Morris Offit, who when taking our weekend winter walks around Pepsi's Sculpture Gardens recommended my writing a book about the many interesting experiences in my exciting retail career.

The book became even more of a family affair with my daughters, Janie N. Lewis and Robin Seegal, and their daughters, Pam and Hallie, serving as my editors and relentless cheerleaders.

Finally, and most importantly, *The Rise of Fashion and Lessons Learned at Bergdorf Goodman* could not have been written without my collaborator and wife, Jackie. Her treasure trove of photos and newspaper clippings made the book possible. Jackie's wisdom, judgment, and encouragement helped mightily to show the magical time in retailing that we had the good fortune to live through. Last, my thanks to my good friend Ann Cohen, who allowed me to use her remarkably beautiful 1930s drawing of Bergdorf Goodman originally printed in *Harper's Bazaar* for the cover of this book.

Thank you to the many players featured in the photographs throughout the book, all of whom contributed to creating the magic of Bergdorf Goodman and the exciting rise of fashion during the sixties, seventies, and eighties.

1

FROM BONWIT TELLER
to
BERGDORF GOODMAN

BONWIT TELLER

My First Job

ONE MONTH BEFORE I interviewed for my
first job at Bonwit Teller, I camped out at the
Hamilton employment agency waiting for an
employment opportunity. It was October 1938.
The world was still in the grip of the Great Depression, and I
had just left high school.

The agency sent me for an interview at the Manufacturers
Hanover Bank and Trust Co. I was required to fill out an
application that looked more like a questionnaire. One of the
questions troubled me; it requested the name and the date
of graduation from high school—but I hadn't graduated. In
fact, except for attending night classes at Erasmus Hall, the
venerable old public high school in Brooklyn from which the
entire secondary school system of New York emerged, I would
have been considered a "high-school dropout."

Badly in need of work, which was very scarce during the
Great Depression, I crossed my fingers, hoped for the best, and
entered a graduation date.

I was hired as a runner. This meant that I was required to
carry a briefcase handcuffed to my wrist and was dispatched
with important business documents to be delivered to various
banks and businesses. I wore a bank uniform and was paid, as

I recall, $15 a week. Lunch was included from a well-stocked cafeteria. I very much enjoyed the professional environment and the executives for whom I worked. All seemed to be going in the right direction, when two weeks later, I received a call from the personnel department.

Before I arrived to meet the executive in charge, I knew the jig was up.

Erasmus Hall had no record of my graduation; hence, I was no longer employed by Hanover Bank and Trust. Nevertheless, a few weeks later I was again sent for an interview. This time the job was with the retailer Bonwit Teller. Lo and behold, a simple application—and no prying questions.

When people asked me years later how I wound up in retailing, I explained, "It was the only job that I could get without taking a test."

LESSON LEARNED

In today's business world, all types of tests are required to determine the qualifications for a job applicant—from clerk to CEO. It is best, as I found out a few years later when I enlisted in the Army Air Corps as an aviation cadet for pilot training, to learn as much as possible about the type of questions and testing that will be asked. There are books and manuals about any subject under the sun. The wise approach? Never go unprepared.

My Introduction to Bonwit Teller

I WAS HIRED as a temporary employee for the busy Christmas holiday season. I began on the day after the elegant 721 Club party. Held to introduce the most elite New York businessmen to exclusive "men only" shopping at the store's new 721 Club, the cocktail party featured the toast of Broadway Mary Martin and the most gorgeous models Bonwit Teller could hire. Now, on the club's first official day of business, I was told to stand in the middle of the floor and courteously guide the male customers, who were not quite comfortable shopping in a women's store, into the newly opened space on the fourth floor.

Before long, the vice president and general manager of Bonwit Teller, William M. Holmes, and the vice president, Abraham Schuel, stepped out of the elevator to inspect the newly opened club. Mr. Archer, the floor manager, whispered into my ear, "That is Mr. Holmes, the vice president and general manager of the store, and Mr. Schuel, the vice president."

In those days there was very little merchandise on the floor. Only a few comfortable sofas, chairs, and T-stands stood across the carpeted floor between the top executives and me.

In one of those "onetime moments," I fortunately had the presence of mind and good manners (and also, I think, even at that young age, opportunism) to say, "Good morning, Mr. Holmes. Good morning, Mr. Schuel."

Both men looked at me as if to say, "Who is this young kid, his first day on the job? He is not only smart enough to say good morning but to mention us by name?"

I had made my first favorable impression in the business world.

That incident left enough of an impression on both men for them to recommend me to what was then called the Personnel Department (now, of course, called Human Resources). Much later I learned that they had told the department to "keep that young fellow on after Christmas and keep an eye on him. He has a future here." So that which began as a temporary Christmas job turned out to be a lifelong business career.

LESSON LEARNED

One of the defining moments of a career is what type of first impression you make on the executives who are instrumental in guiding and deciding your future in the business world.

Higher Education

LEAVING ERASMUS HALL HIGH SCHOOL due to financial needs at home and a less-than-spectacular performance as a student bothered me considerably during my early working days. This feeling quickly disappeared when I was promoted from "door boy" to office boy for Bill Holmes. I was then granted a Bonwit Teller scholarship allowing me to attend college at a night school of my choice. The toss-up was between New York University (NYU) and Columbia.

Always impressed with the Ivy League, even though Columbia was a considerable distance from my home in Brooklyn compared to NYU, I selected night classes at Columbia. Leaving my job at 6:00 p.m., I caught an open-air bus heading up Fifth Avenue. Sitting high on the upper level, I did my homework while surveying my surroundings. The bus passed the Plaza Hotel and proceeded up 59th Street, rolling alongside high-class hotels and apartments on its way up Broadway.

Here I was with a job that had real potential, under the eyes of the general manager of the business, working in one of the best fashion stores in the country. Having left high school to continue my education in a college environment,

I felt that I was sitting on top of the world. The environment captivated me.

But a certain realization set in every time the bus reached Columbia at 115th Street. To keep the Bonwit scholarship, I was expected to achieve more than the passing grades I earned at Erasmus Hall.

Before entering my classes, I ran across Broadway to a candy store that sold cigarettes for a penny each and to Chock Full o'Nuts for a quick sandwich. The cigarettes seemed to calm my nerves enough to help me pass most of my courses with flying colors. (I eventually gave up smoking.)

I must say, I did, however, have moments of regret when I saw the daytime students hanging around their dorms, pitching pennies and shooting the breeze. I felt envious, knowing that I was missing the chance to experience this phase of life and relationships.

LESSON LEARNED

No matter how low the level a position is in starting a career, always look for the bright side of your situation. With ambition and determination, you can achieve the highest goals available in your chosen field.

The Three Pillars of Wisdom:
Building a Career

AT THE VERY BEGINNING of my retail career, I was fortunate, or wise beyond my years, to have the ability to determine which executives would be instrumental to the success of my future in retailing. My "three pillars of wisdom" were Hortense Odlum, president of Bonwit Teller; William (Bill) Holmes, general manager; and Abraham Schuel, treasurer. Each in his or her own way taught me the fundamentals of retailing. They gave me the support I needed to build my own career.

Hortense Odlum was appointed to the presidency of Bonwit Teller by her husband, Floyd Odlum, the head of Atlas Corporation, the investment firm that had acquired the store in 1934. Mrs. Odlum was primarily a homemaker with no retailing experience other than being a customer. She felt that her main contribution would be to meet with the Bonwit Teller customers to find out what they liked about the store, what they didn't like, and equally important, what they as customers would like to see in the store. Her customer luncheons were called the Consumers' Advisory Committee. It was years ahead of the present-day "focus groups."

FROM RIGHT: *William (Bill) Holmes, vice president and general manager; Hortense Odlum, president of Bonwit Teller; and Abraham Schuel, vice president and treasurer. This photograph was taken at Mrs. Odlum's third anniversary party at the store in 1937. (After the war, Hortense Odlum retired and William [Bill] Holmes became president.) In the background is a cake made in the image of Bonwit Teller at 721 Fifth Avenue, now the location of Trump Tower. (Note the inscription from Mr. Holmes in the bottom right corner: "To Ira: With genuine, personal pride in your successful retailing career and all my best wishes always.") (Photo courtesy of Ira Neimark.)*

Mrs. Odlum's committee held one major advantage over the focus group. The committee members spoke directly to the head of the company, which resulted in immediate results when warranted. They were not strangers being paid by research people for opinions later to be presented to a CEO and whomever for some type of action to be taken at some future time.

Mrs. Odlum's other contribution was one of the first direct-mail pieces, called "A Customer's Point of View." The mailing piece depicted the latest fashions carried in the store and was sent to the list of charge customers. (It is no coincidence that Mrs. Odlum's principle of always listening to your customers and taking care of them was shared by another very shrewd and successful housewife-turned-retailer. Beatrice Fox Auerbach became president of G. Fox & Co. about the same time that Mrs. Odlum took the reins at Bonwit Teller. Years later, Mrs. Auerbach would have much to teach me as well.)

From the very beginning I felt I was branded with a hot iron to never forget this basic principle: "Always give the customer what he or she wants."

William Holmes was the consummate merchant. His ability to understand the needs of the Bonwit Teller customer during the Great Depression and to thereby bring the store to the pinnacle of success from 1935 to 1947 was an inspiration to me. So too was his ability to understand his customers' desires, to understand the wholesale apparel and accessory markets, and to interrelate with each and every owner of another company with whom he did business.

Abe Schuel was low-key, quietly managing the finances of Bonwit Teller through the Depression and on to a very profitable period. From Mr. Schuel, I learned inventory management and control down to the last piece of merchandise.

I will never forget two expressions that characterized his philosophy: First, whenever a buyer asked for money beyond his or her merchandise budget, he always said, "For money you can always buy." The second was "Every piece of merchandise is worth money bought to make a profit. Always treat it like money; it has value."

LESSON LEARNED

Always pay close attention to the major executives in your company, particularly those who can teach you something to add to your portfolio of knowledge. It is equally important to make those executives aware of your appreciation for their contribution to your career.

CHANGING OF THE GUARD AT BERGDORF GOODMAN

A Picture's Thousand Words

A PHOTOGRAPH WAS TAKEN of the top executives at Bergdorf Goodman. We sat together in Andrew Goodman's office. It was January 29, 1975, and the occasion was the announcement of my appointment as president and chief executive officer.

Many years after Bergdorf Goodman became one of the leading luxury fashion retailers in the world, I have often looked at this photograph and speculated on what each of the executives in the photo was thinking at that important moment in time.

What Was Andrew Goodman Thinking?

"What could this young fellow coming from B. Altman with a department store background know about running an elegant luxury retailer like Bergdorf Goodman?

"I have led Bergdorf Goodman for the past 25 years, and Father before me built this magnificent business into what it is today. Fortunately, by selling our store to Carter Hawley Hale, I have ensured that what Father and I built will continue for many years to come. I hope Ira Neimark will appreciate what Bergdorf Goodman is, and will concentrate his efforts to improve our problem branch store in White Plains and other Bergdorf Goodman branches in the future."

What Was Leonard Hankin Thinking?

"I have spent my whole career at Bergdorf Goodman, hoping that one day when Andrew Goodman retired, he would, as the owner of the store, appoint me to be his successor.

"Now with the change in ownership, hopefully my appointment as executive vice president will allow me to have the same responsibilities as I had up until now."

What Was Neal Fox Thinking?

"Was it a wise move to leave the position as a general merchandiser at Neiman Marcus, one of the finest specialty stores in the country? Being appointed as executive vice president, general merchandise manager of Bergdorf Goodman, a much smaller store, with Ira Neimark, a young man with a successful retail background, will there be room for me?"

(Within a year, Neal moved on to continue his successful career in retailing, at one point becoming the president of the apparel and accessories retailer Sulka.)

What Was I Thinking?

Andrew Goodman was answering the *Women's Wear Daily* reporter's questions. We felt that one person speaking for the store was best with so many executive changes taking place.

I, as can be seen, was quiet but was thinking of what I knew about Bergdorf Goodman as a store in that highly competitive environment. The conversation swung to Bergdorf Goodman's expansion plans and improving the poor performance of the recently opened Bergdorf's in White Plains, New York.

My thinking then? "Branches, possibly. But the gold mine is right under our feet here at 754 Fifth Avenue."

FROM LEFT TO RIGHT: *Andrew Goodman, Leonard Hankin, Neal Fox, and Ira Neimark. (Photo courtesy of Ira Neimark.)*

I was also thinking back to my days working in Bonwit Teller's luxurious and elegant environment, a very successful high-end luxury retailer, right across Fifth Avenue. I also recalled Bonwit Teller's failures with their branches, and now here was Bergdorf struggling in White Plains.

Better to concentrate on the location closest to customers who, I recalled, wanted first and foremost great assortments of the best and newest fashion merchandise; their concern about the price came second.

In branch stores it would not be possible to have that great assortment. A branch store's emphasis would be on lower prices for suburban customers, not the large assortment of designer merchandise carried in the Fifth Avenue store. This was the direct opposite of the approach that led Bergdorf Goodman to its great success.

I also thought, in order to develop the store to Carter Hawley Hale's expectations and my own, a complete review was necessary to see who our customers were and who we wanted our customers to be in the future.

With Bloomingdales, Saks, and Henri Bendel in the forefront, and Barneys coming up fast, a strategy and an organization was necessary to gain our rightful place as number one not number five.

LESSONS LEARNED

Over the years I have learned that formal press interviews are geared to getting the facts. The people giving the interview should always try to put a positive spin on the discussion.

Sometimes a picture speaks a thousand words.

Bergdorf Goodman's Non-Expansion

I HAVE OFTEN LOOKED BACK to the mid-seventies and eighties at the different store expansion strategies developed by Carter Hawley Hale for its specialty store acquisitions. Its stores were Neiman Marcus, Bergdorf Goodman, and Holt Renfrew in Canada. Carter Hawley Hale was a large, successful department store chain based in California. With great courage and foresight, the chain bought these three retail companies within a few years of each other.

The initial strategy had a few management bumps at Neiman Marcus; these included a number of management changes. But eventually with the appointments of Allen Questrom, then Terry Lundgren, followed by Burt Tansky as CEOs, Neiman Marcus has gone on to great success.

At the celebration in 1979 of Holt Renfrew's Toronto store's $6 million makeover, Stanly Marcus and I were invited to give the Holt Renfrew executives our "words of wisdom." But it was also at this event that one of Carter Hawley Hale's executives, Ardern Batchelder, whispered in my ear, "You fellows at Bergdorf Goodman better make at least $1 million profit this year."

It wasn't Holt Renfrew that I had to worry about. It was Bergdorf Goodman.

Fortunately, after three years of our efforts at Bergdorf Goodman, the critical mass of fashion designers came together and our business, figuratively speaking, took off, creating sales and profits of the highest magnitude.

Part of this success came when Neiman Marcus, with our encouragement, took over Bergdorf Goodman's White Plains branch store. (To offset the negative public relations of Bergdorf Goodman closing its first branch store, a newspaper story indicated that Bergdorf might expand into urban markets, although this was not about to happen. Early on, I learned the essential role the fashion media plays in retail success—or lack thereof—as illustrated by clippings gathered over the years and interspersed throughout this book.)

Looking back, it was Philip Hawley, the CEO of Carter Hawley Hale, whose patience and support with Bergdorf's non-expansion, among many other decisions, was a major contributor to bringing Bergdorf Goodman to the forefront of fashion leadership and to great profitability.

N-M takes BG branch, BG to new markets

By Lisa Anderson

NEW YORK—In a double play within the Carter Hawley Hale organization, Neiman-Marcus will take over Bergdorf Goodman's White Plains branch next fall and Bergdorf's will embark on a multimillion dollar expansion and renovation of its Fifth Ave. flagship and a program of new market entries as early as 1982.

"We very clearly had two successful businesses, each of which has big opportunities, and the way to best acquit the opportunities for each of them was to make this decision," Philip Hawley, president and chief executive officer of Carter Hawley Hale Stores, Inc., said Monday.

Characterizing the move as a "marketing decision," Hawley stressed that in light of Neiman's success in new markets and suburban locations and Bergdorf's strength with the Urban sophisticated fashion customer, this strategy will allow each division to do what it does best.

White Plains represents Neiman's entry into the New York market and, to many observers, signals its vanguard push into the Northeast as part of its stated strategy of becoming a national retailer. Sources say Neiman's expects the White Plains unit to do at least $150 per square foot, or $21 million, in its first year.

The expansion and renovation of Bergdorf's flagship—price-tagged at an estimated $3,500,000 to $5 million—will involve the total store over a period of two to three years. It includes the installation of escalators in the center portion of the store and the addition of 25,000 square feet to the current 100,000 square feet of selling space.

Construction of the escalators, expected to begin next year, will ease traffic flow within the store, which has grown rapidly, last year generating a volume of about $52 million.

The flagship store's strong performance, however, has never been paralleled in its sole branch, White Plains. Opened in October, 1974, the store—with its austere beauty and empty marble expanses—put off casual suburban shoppers, and its enormous 140,000 square feet of space drained profitability.

Neighboring retailers of the store, which is joined to B. Altman by a parking garage, characterized the unit as "a museum of wasted space." Despite efforts of management to warm the interior with visual display and a rearrangement of merchandise last year, and its use of about 10,000 square feet of lower-level space for Bergdorf's catalog operation, the store's volume last year was around $8 million.

"The great success enjoyed by Bergdorf Goodman in New York on Fifth Ave. is not as adaptable to a surburban location," said Ira Neimark, president, noting the White Plains unit "was overspaced for the type of store Bergdorf's is."

Future expansion will be in urban locations, he stressed, and, although he would not be specific, sources indicate Chicago, Boston and Washington, D.C., are among the markets being considered, with Florida and Los Angeles as long-range possibilities.

Bergdorf's will close the White Plains unit in late January, notifying its charge customers of the closing by mail. The store's 150 employees will either be picked up by the flagship store or be hired by Neiman's, which will open around Sept. 1.

An architectural team is being assembled by Neiman's to do a renovation of the store, according to Philip Miller, president of Neiman-Marcus. The unit will be a full-line Neiman-Marcus, he stressed, and will use all existing floor space as well as possibly expanding the selling area to the unit's basement level, which Bergdorf's has been using for services and its catalog operation.

Miller noted preliminary marketing studies done in tandem with Bergdorf's indicate there is a high awareness of the Neiman name in the trading area. He said Bergdorf's charge customers will receive Neiman's cards if they wish.

In a massive expansion program, Neiman Marcus has announced plans which include two more units in the Chicago area, two more in the San Francisco Bay area, two more in the Los Angeles area, one in San Diego, one in Las Vegas and one more in Houston. Sources indicate Neiman's currently is considering locations in the Detroit and Boston areas and that, within the next 12 months, the announcement of additional New York metropolitan branches would be consistent with its recent expansion strategy.

Reprinted with permission from Women's Wear Daily.

LESSONS LEARNED

It is imperative when reviving or developing a business to have the wholehearted support from those who appointed you to that responsibility.

With proper business principles, patience, and fortitude applied to the project, success will be the reward.

The Beginning

THE ANNOUNCEMENT IN JANUARY OF 1975 of my appointment as president of Bergdorf Goodman brought about lifestyle changes. With Bergdorf Goodman's high profile, I was closely watched by the trade press, competition, and others. Who is he and whom does he meet with? What is his lifestyle? This high profile differed with my previous roles at conservative B. Altman and G. Fox in Hartford.

With a much higher profile, I tried (unsuccessfully) to play my new role low-key.

Lunches in G. Fox & Co's Connecticut Room, followed by the famous Charleston Gardens at B. Altman & Co., transformed into grander occasions. Lunches in uptown New York were devoted to meeting the movers and shakers in the fashion industry. The restaurants of choice were Orsini's, 21, La Grenouille, La Côte Basque, and La Caravelle—all within easy walking distance of Bergdorf Goodman.

A good example was my first foray to Orsini's. It was a farewell luncheon for my B. Altman crew. This included Dawn Mello, then fashion director at B. Altman and soon to join Bergdorf Goodman; Helen Galland, president of Bonwit Teller; and Bill Humphreys, the former treasurer of Bonwit

FROM TOP, LEFT TO RIGHT:

*Dawn Mello; Rae Crespin; Ira Neimark;
Geraldine Stutz and Liz Smith; Jack Mulqueen;
Lucy Newhouse and Charles Evans; and Helen
Galland and Bill Humphreys. (Photos by Nick
Machalaba courtesy of* Women's Wear Daily.*)*

Teller. They were possibly discussing Humphreys's next move, soon to be appointed to head Abercrombie & Fitch. Lucy Newhouse, along with Charles Evans, raised lunches to a higher level than just a retailers' gathering. Seventh Avenue entrepreneur Jack Mulqueen, as I recall, had at that time many irons in the fire. Geraldine Stutz, president of Henri Bendel, was the creator of fashion excitement, always ahead of the crowd. Her "Street of Shops" at Bendel was the forerunner of many stores, here and in Europe. Within the store, she installed designer "shops," each specializing in the newest and most exciting merchandise for the sophisticated fashion customers. Geraldine Stutz was a great fashion merchant, who realized long before the other retailers that there were women customers who were looking for new exciting European fashion merchandise.

The Designer Strategy Emerges

The beginning of Bergdorf Goodman's designer strategy began forming at these restaurants. Being privy to these heady times and entrenched in the department store milieu, one of my first questions was this: Why did Henri Bendel, a relatively small specialty store on 57th Street, have all the latest and most exciting European fashion designers and the reputation for being a most exciting store, while Bergdorf Goodman, a much larger store just across the street, have relatively few of the new, exciting designers, and a reputation for not being first with the newest fashions?

As in any successful competitive business strategy, planning and effort had to be made to find the formula to entice many of the fashion designers and customers from Henri Bendel to Bergdorf Goodman directly across 57th Street.

LESSONS LEARNED

In many cases a successful competitor has figured out the necessary steps to become a leader in its particular business. This was true for Henri Bendel across the street as well as Bloomingdales a few blocks away.

The expression "stealing their business" may not be an appropriate or professional expression for a marketing strategy, but that is exactly what had to be done in order for Bergdorf Goodman to become a dominant force as a fashion leader.

The Fifth Avenue Stores

A YEAR OR TWO AFTER I became the CEO of Bergdorf Goodman, *Harper's Bazaar* thought it would be a novel Christmas idea to show the top executives of New York's Fifth Avenue stores along with their choice of the greatest gifts from their stores. (Marvin Traub was included even though Bloomingdales was on Lexington Avenue, because of his store's fashion image.)

Bonwit Teller: George Baylis

George Baylis was one of the long list of retail executives brought in to try to bring the store back to its glory days. After Walter Hoving bought Bonwit Teller from Atlas Corporation in 1947, the list of owners and top executives, too long to list here, tried but never succeeded to achieve that objective. In the early 1980s Donald Trump demolished the Bonwit Teller building in order to build Trump Tower. The store in various forms vanished after that from the retail scene.

Bergdorf Goodman: Ira Neimark

Apropos that I, especially, am shown here on ice skates; I was still trying to get my footing to build Bergdorf Goodman into the leading fashion store on Fifth Avenue.

Bloomingdales: Marvin Traub

Marvin Traub followed in the steps of his boss, Harold Krensky, who initiated Bloomingdales' drive to become a fashionable department store. With the help of Katherine Murphy, Bloomingdales' fashion director, Marvin Traub made Bloomingdales into one of the first destination department stores for the younger, trendy fashion customer. After his retirement, he went on to become a very successful business consultant.

B. Altman & Co.: John Christian

John Christian became the general merchandise manager and then president of B. Altman after the retirement of Randy Stambaugh, the executive who brought me back to New York. Unfortunately, not many years after John's appointment, due to an IRS ruling, B. Altman was sold. The store continued to decline and was eventually closed. The wonderful B. Altman building on Fifth Avenue and 34th Street is now the home of a major annex of the New York Public Library.

Lord & Taylor: Harry Murray

A perfect gentleman, Harry Murray was the only retailer who wrote a letter of welcome to me when I returned to New York from New England. I didn't get to know Harry Murray very well once he retired from Lord & Taylor shortly after I became the CEO of Bergdorf Goodman. His retirement moved Bill Lippincott up to chairman. It was then that Bill Arnold, the head of Lord & Taylor's owner, Associated Dry Goods, approached me to become the president of Lord & Taylor. I obviously declined that great opportunity. Since I hadn't been in my new position at Bergdorf Goodman even six months, moving to another store would have broken faith with my new employer, Carter Hawley Hale.

FROM LEFT TO RIGHT: *George Baylis, Ira Neimark, Marvin Traub, John Christian, Harry Murray, Norman Wechsler, and Harry Platt in a* Harper's Bazaar *Christmas special article.*

I. Magnin: Norman Wechsler

Norman Wechsler had previously been the president of Saks Fifth Avenue, qualifying him to be included in this lineup. At I. Magnin, Norman Wechsler opened 24 stores. He retired in 1981. A number of years later after a number of management changes, I. Magnin was liquidated.

Tiffany & Co: Harry Platt

If anyone personified the elegance of Fifth Avenue, it was Harry Platt. He raised the fashion profile of Tiffany, as well as the sales. His strategic expansion has been a great success, continued today by his astute successors.

LESSON LEARNED

Retail stores, like human beings, go through various stages of life. Some achieve success and high profiles and eventually pass on to oblivion in what would be considered a lifetime. A few go on, it seems, forever. The corporate entity that owns and operates the stores is critical to the strategy and direction the store will take. I have often compared the heads of the stores to ship captains. Success and long-term viability depend on how skillfully chief executives guide their stores through rough weather, understanding that without paying attention to retail fundamentals and basic retail principles, they will eventually wind up on the rocks.

Reinventing Retailing

THE STRATEGY OF CONVERTING Bergdorf Goodman to the highest fashion name store on Fifth Avenue required reinventing the merchandise and marketing concept. This was the key for the store as well as the fashion designers who were beginning to be recognized by the fashion customers.

The timing of my arrival at Bergdorf Goodman in the early seventies was fortuitous for the initial development of my strategy. During the sixties and early seventies the fashion designers in New York, Paris, and Milan began to develop into highly recognizable fashion entities.

At this point it is important to note that most of the important designer fashion collections were carried in all the major New York stores, from Barneys downtown to Bloomindales uptown and other fashion retailers in between. All except for Bergdorf Goodman. Again, fortunately for me, these other major stores did not aggressively promote the designer lines. I wondered if this was my opportunity.

In 1975 I went to the French couture shows on my first European trip for Bergdorf Goodman. I realized then and there what an enormous impact Yves Saint Laurent would make with his Russian Peasant couture collection.

FROM LEFT TO RIGHT: *Maxime de la Falaise in a skirt of her own creation talking to Marina Schiano in a gold Yves Saint Laurent look at Regine's in New York for a before and after party and group bus trip to the Muhammad Ali vs. Ken Norton boxing match, September 20, 1976. (Photo by Karlin Lynn courtesy of* Women's Wear Daily.*) Pilar Echavarria at the 1977 Fendi fur collection event. (Photo by Rubin Darleen courtesy of* Women's Wear Daily.*)*

My reinventing strategy began to take shape.

The objective quickly became clear. Bergdorf Goodman must not only attract every important French, Italian, and American fashion designer but also we would aggressively and dramatically promote these fashion designers with extravagant and elaborate fashion shows in order to make their names and Bergdorf Goodman synonymous with the most exciting designer merchandise available under one roof. Every important designer would have his or her own important shop, designed by the designer, at a prime location in the store.

Dramatic and newsworthy fashion shows would attract the fashion press from the United States, Paris, Milan, and London. The fashion press would play an essential role in the strategy not only by providing free promotion for these shows and their featured designers but also by offering us a steady source of impartial criticism; some may have taken offense at this criticism, but we at Bergdorf Goodman took it as an opportunity, examining it as though holding up a mirror to see how we might adjust our image to the best advantage. We would hold these glamorous and often star-studded events at landmarks such as Studio 54, the ice-skating rink at Radio City (notably for Armani), the Crystal Palace, the World Trade Center (Lacroix), the 71st Street Armory (Montana), and the Pulitzer Fountain (Fendi and Calvin Klein), to name just a few. The fashion press covered all of these events, propelling the

FROM LEFT TO RIGHT: *Sister Parish at the 1977 Fendi fur collection event; Nina Hunter at the 1977 Fendi fur collection event. (Photos by Rubin Darleen courtesy of* Women's Wear Daily.*)*

Diana Vreeland (at left) at the 1977 Fendi fur collection event at Bergdorf Goodman.
(Photo by Rubin Darleen courtesy of Women's Wear Daily.*)*

fashion designers to front-page news and carrying Bergdorf Goodman along with them. Fifth Avenue windows and newspaper advertising with feature ads in *The New York Times*, *Vogue*, and *Harper's Bazaar* were the additional promotions to help make the fashion designers "branded names."

When our merchandising strategy was in full swing, all of the successful fashion designers heretofore known and carried only in our competitors' stores were catapulted into fame and fortune. This, of course, was because Bergdorf Goodman promoted them so aggressively. It was no coincidence that Bergdorf Goodman became increasingly associated with the fame and fortune of these designers and this association was to eclipse that of our competitors.

For the designers and Bergdorf Goodman it was a win–win strategy. For the competition? Enough said.

LESSONS LEARNED

Customers are always looking for something new to make their lives a bit more exciting, no matter what age or gender, in good times or bad. It has ever been thus and will continue, since fashion-conscious customers are always looking to enhance their lives and make them more glamorous.

Businesspeople must always recognize the customer is looking to satisfy his or her desires; otherwise, their businesses will never achieve the great success that is available to them.

Pockets of Blandness

A S HERBERT MINES, the head of Business Careers, a major executive recruiter, pointed out in the mid-seventies, "The sales and profit performance of the major retailers of that time required the owners to make top management changes." By November 1975, a *Women's Wear Daily* article announced that except for Bloomingdales and Bendel's, "The Fifth Avenue stores failed to acknowledge the winds of change." Here was a perfect example of our strategy's unofficial partnership with the impartial fashion press. In this article, the description of Bergdorf Goodman's progress was overall very positive, except for one note in the last paragraph: "In the process of all this reorganization the store's floors have become more fluid and inviting. There are still 'pockets of blandness,' but by and large, Bergdorf's is beginning to generate the kind of excitement that marks it as a store to be watched."

Well! We were very pleased with the positive aspects of the article. However, we were disappointed to learn that with all of our initial efforts to upgrade the store to be competitive with our retail rivals, we had, according to the leading fashion newspaper, failed to receive a top grade. We went through every corner of the store to identify these "pockets of blandness" and made the corrections we thought necessary. Then we invited the reporter back to see if we passed.

Pass we did, and we continued to improve every day, every week, every month, and every year to reach the approval of our customers, our suppliers, and the fashion press in order to be the top fashion retailer in New York City and eventually the entire United States.

I am pleased to say, this article went on to say of one of our competitors, Bonwit Teller, "It is still plagued with lack of focus." The other Fifth Avenue stores didn't come off very well either.

Objectives and Strategy

THE YEARS 1975 THROUGH 1976 was a very busy time for Bergdorf Goodman. The fashion press was quick to point out that a new direction was required to bring the store into the mainstream of those and future years of high-fashion merchandising. As in most business takeovers, when the holding company tries to appease the former owner by keeping the organization together while bringing in a new management team, organizational problems are quick to develop.

With Andrew Goodman as chairman and myself as president, Neal Fox was brought in from Neiman Marcus to be executive vice president. Leonard Hankin remained executive vice president. Dawn Mello was brought in at that point to become fashion director. Not surprisingly, a Wednesday, February 14, 1975, *Women's Wear Daily* article, titled "Objectives and Strategy," picked up the story and pointed out, "Some trade observers noted that there was a duplication of talent. This too has resulted in some conflict."

Observing a relatively small business with a great potential down the road, the *Women's Wear Daily* article was very accurate. Neal Fox, a very capable merchant, was put in an untenable position and made plans to move on to another successful retail career. By coincidence, the same day, *Women's Wear Daily* also pointed out that Richard Hauser, the chairman of Neiman Marcus, declined the offer to become president of Saks Fifth Avenue.

My mission was clear. Again, as the *Women's Wear Daily* article said, "Some market observers feel Bergdorf's lost sight of what was happening. As one put it, during the entire sportswear explosion, they went on selling dresses."

It didn't require a rocket scientist to immediately expand the Misses Sportswear Department, with key designers like Calvin Klein growing their business tenfold in one year. *Women's Wear Daily* had it right from the beginning—and we were paying attention.

The Italian Designers

IN MANY CASES, luck and timing can do more to achieve business success than good planning with poor timing and no luck. The best example of this was demonstrated with Bergdorf Goodman's Italian strategy, developed by Dawn Mello, at that time Bergdorf's fashion director. I first met Dawn Mello in 1968, when she was the fashion director of the May Department Stores Buying Office. It didn't take me long to realize Dawn had "the eye." Dawn was able to demonstrate that she could spot a trend or a designer early on. She proved this when I brought her to B. Altman, and again at Bergdorf Goodman, where she identified the early potential of the Italian ready-to-wear designers.

Bergdorf's good luck and mine began with my arrival in 1975 when the French couture was making fashion headlines, and to my knowledge, none of the American retailers were interested in promoting that fashion opportunity. On one of my first visits to Europe for Bergdorf Goodman, I became aware of the excitement that the French couture generated among the fashion press and the world's wealthiest and most fashionable women. I had been particularly impressed with Yves Saint Laurent's Russian costume collection, as was the fashion press. It was then that the timing was right for the

Fendi fur collection, 1977, at Bergdorf Goodman. (Photos by Rubin Darleen courtesy of Women's Wear Daily.)

French couture to be reintroduced to America by Bergdorf Goodman. With heavy lobbying, Yves Saint Laurent decided to sell his collection to Bergdorf Goodman, which opened the French ready-to-wear collections to us.

At the same time Italian couture such as Valentino was at the forefront of fashion. André Laug, Mila Schoen, and others wanted to be recognized by Bergdorf Goodman as well. We didn't let them down and also brought them on board.

The magical mix of French and Italian couture coming to Bergdorf precisely as we brought in the newly emerging Italian ready-to-wear was key. Bergdorf Goodman was then catapulted into the fashion headlines. The timing was very fortunate, with the wonderful Italian ready-to-wear as fashion leaders, and we put our Italian strategy into play.

However, there were challenges in the beginning. Previous to my arrival at Bergdorf Goodman, our competition—Henri Bendel, Bloomingdales, Saks Fifth Avenue, and Barneys—had all been successful early buyers in the Italian market, whereas, to the Italians, it seemed that Bergdorf Goodman was to be ignored. The key to turning this negative situation around, we felt, was the Fendi family. With the French ready-to-wear designers, it was Yves Saint Laurent's decision, after heavy lobbying, to sell his collection to Bergdorf Goodman that opened the French ready-to-wear collections to us. The Fendi family played this role for the Italian designers.

The many meetings in Rome with the five Fendi sisters and their representatives, Count Savorelli and Count Rudi Crespi, brought Fendi into the fold. One by one, then two by two, nearly all the important Italian designers who came to Bergdorf's became stars due to the many extravagant fashion shows, newspaper and magazine advertisements, and Fifth Avenue window displays. These efforts raised their profiles to become international fashion leaders.

LESSONS LEARNED
No matter what the class of merchandise, to be successful in the luxury fashion business, customers must feel that they are being sold the newest and most exciting merchandise available.

Good luck and timing often help to achieve your objectives.

The Shops for European Collections

B Y 1977, after Bergdorf Goodman's dramatic and surprise reintroduction of the French couture to America, *Women's Wear Daily*'s reporters asked the important question: Which of the five major Fifth Avenue stores would be first in fashion leadership in a very competitive environment?

A *Women's Wear Daily* headline in September of that year, "Five on Fifth: Who's on First," was enough to keep the competitive juices flowing.

To maintain its own momentum, Bergdorf Goodman announced its next big fashion statement. A series of boutiques called the European Collections would open in March of that year. This move pushed Bergdorf a bit further ahead of its direct Fifth Avenue competition, which at that time consisted of Bonwit Teller, Saks Fifth Avenue, Lord & Taylor, and B. Altman & Co. There was still a way to go in order to catch up to Henri Bendel and Bloomingdales.

Another instant reaction to all the favorable press and the high-profile fashion customers' attention were two calls from Paris. Jean-Louis Dumas, the new head of Hermès, and Dennis Colban, the owner of Charvet, requested appointments to discuss setting up their shops in Bergdorf Goodman.

Bergdorf European in-store collections: Mila Schoen. (Photo by Rubin Darleen courtesy of Women's Wear Daily.*)*

Bergdorf European in-store collections: Saint Laurent Rive Gauche. (Photo by Rubin Darleen courtesy of Women's Wear Daily.*)*

Bergdorf European in-store collections: Fendi. (Photo by Rubin Darleen courtesy of Women's Wear Daily.*)*

Bergdorf European in-store collections: Geoffrey Beene. (Photo by Rubin Darleen courtesy of Women's Wear Daily.*)*

With the objective of fashion leadership in mind, a new fashion office was formed, headed by Dawn Mello. The job description of the office in its simplest terms was like that of a three-legged stool. The first leg was the responsibility of the fashion office to shop thoroughly all the important fashion markets in the United States, Paris, Milan, and Rome. The second leg was the responsibility of the Bergdorf buyers to the fashion office's direction, the purpose being to have one fashion point of view, not a scattering of various buyers' judgments. The third leg was the additional responsibility of the fashion office to identify the newest and the most exciting designer merchandise to be displayed in the Fifth Avenue windows, fashion shows, and newspaper and magazine advertising. This three-legged strategy naturally included maintaining our close contact with the fashion press.

This consistent and unified approach helped to move Bergdorf Goodman closer to its goal to become the first on Fifth.

LESSONS LEARNED

A sound and imaginative marketing strategy is the first important step for a business to grow to its potential.

It is critical to have a professional and talented organization, no matter how large or small, with a specific direction of the company's objectives.

Barneys and the End of Fashion Designer Exclusivity

A NUMBER OF YEARS AGO I received a call from David Bonderman, the CEO of Texas Pacific. He had not been aware that I was the father-in-law of Fred Seegal, my daughter Robin's husband, who at that time was the president of Wasserstein Perella. Texas Pacific was interested in examining Barneys, who had entered Chapter 11, due to the Pressman family's overexpansion as well as their serious financial problems. Fred told Mr. Bonderman of my retail background as CEO of Bergdorf Goodman and thought that I would be able to help him with his due diligence examination of Barneys.

There were two reasons why I accepted the assignment. First, I felt well qualified for this type of project. Second, I welcomed the opportunity to study the merchandising of Barneys. Fierce competitor that they were, I admired Fred Pressman for being an outstanding merchant.

It was a bit awkward for Gene and Bob Pressman and the management of Barneys to meet me under such difficult circumstances. Bergdorf Goodman and I were considered their nemesis.

Fred Pressman died in 1996. Previous to his death, he handed over to his sons, Gene and Bob, the responsibility of running the store. The retail history of the financial and real-estate circumstances for the family to lose control of the store is well documented, and not necessary for me to go into in explaining my advisory assignment.

In the 1970s and 1980s Bergdorf Goodman negotiated with different fashion designers for exclusive or semi-exclusive arrangements as to who would be featured in the store, as well as the size and the location of their departments. It was critical to me to have the fashion lines, where possible, ideally first-exclusive with Bergdorf Goodman. Second, if not exclusive, then limited distribution to Saks Fifth Avenue or Bloomingdales, not both. If a designer required a third store, we would recommend Barneys, downtown on 17th Street. We knew that the approach of giving the designer lines to Barneys would come back to haunt us one day. When Barneys moved uptown to Madison Avenue, it did.

This meant that our exclusive and semi-exclusive strategy of two stores uptown carrying the top fashion lines was broadened to three, and not long after, Bergdorf Goodman, Saks Fifth Avenue, Bloomingdales, and Barneys all carried, in most cases, the same designer lines. The era of designer exclusivity was over.

It was not difficult to see, with the proper management in place, that Barneys could be a very successful retail entity on Madison Avenue. In a relatively brief due diligence summary, I recommended to Texas Pacific their acquisition of Barneys.

From a merchandising point of view, in my opinion, this would have been an excellent retail opportunity for them, both in sales and profits. In addition to my input, Texas Pacific employed accounting firms that supplied the financial side of the due diligence. Whatever they recommended, Texas Pacific passed on the acquisition. Two other investment houses took

over, moving Barneys out of Chapter 11. Barneys has gone on
to great success under the direction of Howard Socol as CEO.

In 2005, Texas Pacific, with the private equity firm Warburg
Pincus, bought The Neiman Marcus Group from the Smith
family, who in 1987, as General Cinema, bought Neiman
Marcus and Bergdorf Goodman from Carter Hawley Hale.

Life can be like a pinball: You can never be sure where the
ball may bounce.

I often wonder what the retail landscape would look like
today if Texas Pacific had followed my recommendation to
buy Barneys when it was in bankruptcy.

LESSON LEARNED
When a financial company is considering an acquisition of a
retailer, financial advisors present one side of the equation. A
merchandise advisor might present another side. Both should
be evaluated carefully in order to arrive at the right decision.

New York: The Changing Scene

I HAD THE OPPORTUNITY to be a participant and an observer of the changes taking place in the rarified atmosphere of upper Fifth Avenue and Madison Avenue. The Pressman family moving Barneys from Seventh Avenue and 17th Street to Madison Avenue and 62nd Street was a very ambitious, aggressive, and dramatic shift in New York retailing.

Unfortunately, for the Pressman family, financial problems led the store into bankruptcy and a change of ownership.

LESSONS LEARNED

Moving a wonderful and successful retail establishment is fraught with peril.

Barneys possibly could have maintained its very successful retail store on 17th Street as well as opening on Madison. Manhattan is large enough to have a downtown store as well as uptown.

EXTRAORDINARY TIMES

Fun and Games in Paris

I FIRST BECAME AWARE of Paris when I was six years old. Not through history or geography books, but in 1927 when Charles Lindbergh flew over the Atlantic Ocean solo to Paris in 33 and a half hours. Everyone in America, France, and the rest of the world was excited. So much so that when my father took me and my brother, Lester, to see the ticker-tape welcome–home parade for "Lucky Lindy" on Broadway, due to the tremendous crowds, we couldn't get within two blocks of the street. We still went home with an unforgettable memory of that eventful day.

Later on at school, when I learned the history of France and especially Paris, little did I know how important a role Paris would play many years later in my business career.

Back in 1938, when I became the office boy to the then vice president and general manager of Bonwit Teller, Bill Holmes, I became aware of Paris once again when he traveled to France by ocean liner. We heard he didn't like the red carpet in his suite on board, so it was changed to green, for good luck. A true Irishman to the core.

Following that, Roy Rudolph, the president of Bonwit Teller, who succeeded Bill Holmes, made his ocean voyage in 1948 to France and on to Paris. Among his many responsibilities on the trip, he met a new, young fashion designer named Hubert Givenchy. Although still a very junior executive, I was invited to his bon voyage party aboard his steamship and brought along a small bottle of champagne as a gift. Ten years later I would listen to Beatrice Fox Auerbach, the owner of Hartford, Connecticut's G. Fox & Co., describe the many visits to Paris she and her family made.

Finally, at long last, came my own trip to Paris in 1967. I was ready and anxious to make this first trip to what was and still is the legendary City of Light. I was traveling for G. Fox & Co. It was to be the first of many during the next 25 years. (My brother, Lester, beat me to it. He arrived with the first wave at Utah Beach in Normandy on June 6, 1944, courtesy of the 4th Division, U.S. Army.)

In 1967, Pan Am's Boeing 747 was the transportation of choice, followed by my first Air France's Concorde flight in 1976. This was quite a difference from the days when my predecessors traveled luxuriously by steamship. The difference? Travel then was slow and elegant instead of fast and elegant.

Of course, all our traveling and meeting with the French fashion designers was to convince them that their presentation and introduction to the American fashion public via Bergdorf Goodman would enhance their reputations; naturally, we would achieve this by promoting them far more than our competition.

As an example, Dawn Mello and I had a major breakthrough when we had a luncheon meeting with Claude Montana at Restaurant Le Voltaire, owned by the same family since 1939, at 27 Quai Voltaire. We were able to convince Montana to commit to an exclusive arrangement of his collections at Bergdorf Goodman. It was a great success story when he and his collection arrived in New York. The lunches and dinners at the important restaurants in Paris helped to familiarize us with the famous French and even the Italian fashion designers, and they to us.

One of my earliest discoveries and most enjoyable restaurants was L'Orangerie, on the Left Bank. My wife, Jackie, and I had our first of many dinners there going back to 1970. Back then, Ferris Megarity, the head of publicity for B. Altman, told me of this small, elegant restaurant where the food was great, the price was right, and you would never get sick. He was pleased to see that we followed his advice.

Over the years many fashion celebrities we would come to know would be found there any night of the week—Yves Saint Laurent, Emanuel Ungaro, Count and Countess Hubert d'Ornano, to name a few. This is another example of how in the luxurious Paris environment, I became familiar with the great French designers and their collections that they brought to Bergdorf Goodman that helped move the store to the forefront of luxury fashion retailing.

LESSON LEARNED
Everyone has a desire to visit the great cities of the world. With hard work, patience, and fortitude, this dream can be achieved. The visit is made more worthwhile by finding and engaging international talent.

Dancing with Celebrities: Partying at Maxim's in Paris

AS IT MY GOOD LUCK, having the pinball bounce in the right direction, or great timing on my part?

Immediately after I joined Bergdorf Goodman, the need to bring the store back to what was relevant, exciting, and newsworthy in the world of fashion was paramount in my thinking. My inspiration from Yves Saint Laurent's fall couture collection presented in Paris in the spring of 1975 brought about one of the most dramatic reemergences of any retailer in the fashion business.

Fortunately, Eugenia Sheppard, considered at that time the doyenne of the fashion writers, was a very strong believer and promoter of French couture. No sooner had I announced my plan to bring French couture, consisting of Yves Saint Laurent, Christian Dior, and Hubert Givenchy, to Bergdorf Goodman in New York than Eugenia began writing about the importance of French couture as an influence on all fashion creativity at every level.

At that time, Eugenia Sheppard wrote for the *International Herald Tribune* and the *New York Post*. She was also syndicated in newspapers all over the United States. When she mentioned

New York Post *fashion columnist Eugenia Sheppard (center) with Dior designer Marc Bohan, Princess Caroline's fiancé Philippe Junot, Prince Albert, Princess Grace, and Princess Caroline of Monaco* (left to right). *(Photo courtesy of* The New York Post.*)*

New York Post *fashion columnist Eugenia Sheppard talks with fashion designer Pierre Cardin at a party honoring her at Maxim's. (Photo courtesy of* The New York Post.*)*

Bergdorf Goodman as the only retailer in America presenting French couture, we became the instant fashion star.

In January 1978, Ms. Sheppard invited me to a party at Maxim's in Paris due to Bergdorf Goodman's representation of French couture in America. The party was held by the French couture industry in honor of Ms. Sheppard's contribution to couture. At this event, I met all the important French fashion designers. Two of my most memorable moments at the party were dancing with Eugenia and meeting Princess Grace of Monaco and her daughter Princess Caroline.

New York Post *fashion columnist Eugenia Sheppard gets a kiss from fashion designer Marc Bohan of the house of Dior at a party honoring her at Maxim's. (Photo courtesy of* The New York Post.*)*

New York Post *fashion columnist Eugenia Sheppard dances with Ira Neimark, president of Bergdorf Goodman, during a party honoring her at Maxim's. (Photo courtesy of* The New York Post.*)*

This event and many to follow catapulted Bergdorf Goodman into the front ranks as the fashion leader, attracting crowds of fashion-conscious customers and confounding our competition.

LESSON LEARNED

When a business has lost its position of leadership in any industry, it is imperative for that business to change direction in order to capture the attention of lost customers as well as to attract a new audience.

Parties, Parties, Parties

I N THE EARLY SEVENTIES, the luxury fashion designers and upscale retailers recognized that large fashion shows and elegant parties would bring about an undreamed-of amount of favorable newspaper coverage and larger sales. For many years prior to the European fashion designers' explosion, luxury specialty stores such as Bergdorf Goodman held small exclusive fashion shows with the funds donated to society's favorite charity of that time.

One such occasion was held in May 1975, two months after I joined Bergdorf Goodman. The fashion show was held on the St. Regis Roof, for a select group of high-profile society ladies, including Nan Kempner, Pat Buckley, Nancy Kissinger, Françoise de la Renta, and Dina Merrill, just to name a few.

Jo Hughes, Bergdorf Goodman's "saleslady to society," had great influence with the fashion designers. With her small, select fashion shows, she could summon the designers and her imposing guest list by intimidating them simply by advising them "not to be left out." Some of the designers featured included Halston, Donald Brooks, Oscar de la Renta, Bill Blass, and Geoffrey Beene.

Jerry Zipkin, Pat Buckley, and Nan Kempner at Jo Hughes's 1975 summer luncheon fashion fund-raiser for the Musicians Emergency Fund. (Photo by Simins Peter courtesy of Women's Wear Daily.*)*

Estée Lauder, Ira Neimark, and Nicky Lane at Jo Hughes's 1975 summer luncheon fashion fund-raiser for the Musicians Emergency Fund. (Photo by Simins Peter courtesy of Women's Wear Daily.*)*

Jo Hughes and Donald Brooks at Jo Hughes's 1975 summer luncheon fashion fund-raiser for the Musicians Emergency Fund. (Photo by Simins Peter courtesy of Women's Wear Daily.)

I arrived on the scene two months prior to this show and immediately had a number of questions about the show. Why was this a must-attend event? Some ladies on their own would visit their favorite designer's showroom and buy at a private customer's discount, or in some cases, be given their selection as a gift. These high-profile ladies had their photographs taken in their favorite designer's clothes. This, of course, was very good public relations for the designer and was the forerunner of today's Academy Awards red-carpet fashion extravaganza.

For the fashion designers, it was an inexpensive ride to have their names and new season's merchandise publicized by Bergdorf Goodman's elite customer list.

For the fashion designers, it was an inexpensive ride to have their names and new season's merchandise publicized by Bergdorf Goodman's elite customers—from society events onto the pages of the major fashion press ("30 Years," Women's Wear Daily, *September 22, 1977).*

CLOCKWISE FROM TOP LEFT: *Irwin Alfin; Estée and Joseph Lauder; Paul Woolard; Alain Wertheimer; Geoffrey Beene; Jackie and Ira Neimark; Richard Salomon, Mark Laracy, and Marty Schmidt; Mike Gibbons and Carol Phillips; Sylvie Chanteuille; and Patrick and Claudia de Givenchy.*

In September 1983 Chanel had its first boutique and couture fashion show in many years in the United States at Bergdorf Goodman. The show was held in Bergdorf Goodman as a charity event for the School of American Ballet. For such events, the charity sold the tickets to benefit the charity. Bergdorf Goodman (and other retailers), at its own expense, hosted the benefit in a dramatic way, and the store would benefit from the publicity. This approach allowed the ladies to do some serious shopping, since the show, the merchandise, and the salespeople were all in the store and not in a hotel or a public arena.

One designer showing his or her complete collection is much more effective for sales than a few designers showing a few styles. The audience is large enough even if a few of the customers chose to defect and shop the designer's showroom (Chanel frowned on that practice). These shows attracted serious customers such as Kathleen Hearst, Anne Bass, Nina Griscom, and Ivana Trump.

LESSON LEARNED
Customers interested in luxury merchandise can tell the difference between when a fashion show is geared for public relations and when it is arranged for serious business. The sales figures at these events proved it.

Parties and Beyond

STARTING IN THE SEVENTIES and eighties with the emergence of the American fashion designers in New York and the influx of the European fashion designers to the city, the high-profile charity events seemed to be events worthwhile even by today's standards. An elegant party seemed to be held in an elegant venue every night of the week.

Examples of society parties and business events that were newsworthy and important enough to be given strong press presentations include the following events.

November 1984, The Metropolitan Club
Emanuel Ungaro and Anouk Aimée celebrated the official launch of the designer's fragrance, Diva, at Bergdorf Goodman. The evening's hostesses were Nan Kempner and Mica Ertegun. The evening's guests included Doris Duke, Ann Getty, Joanne Herring, Norma Dana, Freddie and Isabel Eberstadt, Shakira and Michael Caine, Judy Peabody, and Anne Johnson.

Doris Duke (left) and Ann Getty (right) at the 1984 Ungaro Diva perfume launch. (Photo courtesy of Women's Wear Daily.*)*

Ira and Jackie Neimark (left) and Isabel and Freddie Eberstadt (right) at the 1984 Ungaro Diva perfume launch. (Photos courtesy of Women's Wear Daily.*)*

Shakira Caine and Michael Caine at the 1984 Ungaro Diva perfume launch.
(Photos courtesy of Women's Wear Daily.*)*

Bianca Jagger and Duchess Offeria (right) at the 1984 Ungaro Diva perfume launch. (Photos courtesy of Women's Wear Daily.)

November 1985, The Seventh Regiment Armory

This evening celebrated the 10th anniversary of the American Division of Bidermann Industries. The company had been a successful manufacturer of many American brands of merchandise—such as Ralph Lauren and Calvin Klein—and in Europe the major manufacturer of Yves Saint Laurent's Rive Gauche. The guests numbered approximately a thousand. The theme was a traditional Moroccan dinner. Guests included Joan Fontaine, Regine, Robert Joffrey, and Dalia and Larry Leeds.

"If the American division of your company was approaching the end of its first decade and your wife had been raised in Morocco, is there any doubt what the theme of your tenth anniversary would be? For Maurice Z. Bidermann, founder of Bidermann Industries, the Paris-based apparel giant, there was never any question, except perhaps whether to offer silverware during the second course of the traditional Moroccan feast. (He did.)" So went the lead of "Tres Sheik," Women's Wear Daily's Friday, November 4, 1983 coverage of Biderrmann's fête for wife Danielle, which included caterers du jour, Hollywood stars, social celebrities, a world premiere from the Joffrey ballet, a $270,000 tab, and fashion, fashion, fashion.

Italian Fashion Stories

THE TIMING OF MY INTRODUCTION to the world of Italian fashion was again for me a great deal of luck. My first visit to the fashion markets of Europe for G. Fox & Co. was in 1967, followed by my trips for B. Altman & Co. in 1970. Those early visits prepared me for the emergence of the new important Italian collections for Bergdorf Goodman in 1975. Once again in my career, the pinball bounced in the right direction.

My early trips for G. Fox gave me an overall exposure to the moderate and upscale markets in Italy, particularly in fashion accessories, knits, and leather goods. G. Fox was associated with the Macy/May Co. buying office that unfortunately did not inspire me to explore the luxury markets.

On the other hand, B. Altman, being associated with the Giorgini Italian buying office, was a completely different story. The office associated with B. Altman was upscale. It was run by Gianni Ghini with his associate Matilde Giorgini, the daughter of Giovanni Giorgini—the man known as the "Godfather of Italian Fashion." On February 12, 1951, Giovanni had organized the first Italian fashion show at his villa in Florence. Enormously successful, the event, which featured 180 collections, became known as the birth of Italian fashion.

My arrival in Italy in 1970 coincided with the rivalry between Rome and Milan. It was agreed that the high-fashion, or couture, designers would show in Rome in January and July. The ready-to-wear collections would be shown in Milan, April and October.

In order to build B. Altman's underdeveloped fashion business, our fashion director, Dawn Mello, recommended sampling some of the new Italian ready-to-wear collections. Krizia was one of the first, an instant success.

It wasn't until I arrived at Bergdorf Goodman a few years later that the Italian ready-to-wear was in full swing. Now I was ready to move forward.

My first visits to Rome were for the Italian couture. I was particularly interested in Mila Schoen. I won't go into the details of her merchandise other than to say her clothes were elegant classics, meticulously made, luxurious, and expensive—an easy sell to the right customers. With a great deal of persuasion, I convinced Madame Schoen to confine her collection to Bergdorf Goodman in New York—the first of many more exclusives to come. I also attended the couture shows of Valentino, André Laug, and others, which enabled me to compare the Italian with the French couture the following week in Paris.

Once we reintroduced the French couture at Bergdorf Goodman and got a great deal of attention from the fashion press, Dawn Mello's Italian strategy was introduced. I must say, Mr. Giorgini would have been proud of us. In addition to the Italian high-fashion collections of Mila Schoen, Valentino, André Laug, and Gianni Versace, just to name a few, we bought heavily into the ready-to-wear collections of Krizia, Fendi, Basile, Giorgio Armani, Nino Cerruti, Ferragamo, and Gianfranco Ferré.

With that most impressive lineup of the Italian collections, the French and American designers wanted to come on board as well.

Dawn Mello acted as editor, not only of the collections that we should carry but also in directing her staff to work with our buyers to create the Bergdorf Goodman point of view. Dawn said, "It is not what you carry, it's what you don't carry that makes us a fashion store." This held true.

"A Small Party with Friends"

We wedged into our visits to cities and fashion shows times for a bit of relaxation as well. In 1978, in between the Italian couture fashion shows in Rome and the French couture shows that were held a few days later in Paris, Aldo Pinto, the president of Krizia, invited me to play golf in Sardinia. I stayed at the fabulous Hotel Cala Di Volpe and played at, I believe, the Pevero Golf Club nearby.

One beautiful summer evening, Aldo and his wife, Mariuccia, invited me to their home in Porto Cervo, a beautiful setting. Only the Italians delightfully refer to a gathering such as this as "a small party with some friends." At the "small party" sleek boats pulled up to the shore, many piloted by a crew of one or two, with one in a barman's white jacket, serving cocktails to the owners and a few of their guests.

I began to realize what was meant by the Italian expression *La dolce vita*. As the guests gathered around the dinner tables, Aldo and his sous chefs prepared the largest pot of pasta that I have ever seen. Oh, how the wine and conversation flowed! Italian hospitality made me wish that I could speak the language to join in the hilarious conversations.

There were, as the saying goes, a lot of "beautiful people." One of Mariuccia's relatives was Franco Rosi, a film director. He introduced me to the gorgeous Italian movie actress Virna Lisi and lo and behold arranged for her to sit next to me. This was a great evening, not to be forgotten.

Next stop, Paris.

LESSON LEARNED
There is a time for business and a time for fun. Both must be treated accordingly. Business relationships are just that. Beatrice Auerbach Fox's rule was this: Never accept a gift that could not be consumed or eaten at one sitting. This is still good advice.

Fashionable Events

AMERICAN AND EUROPEAN fashion designers, manufacturers, wholesalers, and retailers, recognizing that the Academy Awards in Hollywood brought great attention to the movie business, were not to be outdone. Possibly one of the first events following that format was the Council of Fashion Designers of America Awards, better known as the CFDA. A two-page spread under the tongue-in-cheek headline "Louise Faces the Fashion Flakes" covered the 1982 awards. "Louise" was Louise Esterhazy, nom de plume of a mythical fashion reporter for *Women's Wear Daily*.

Not unlike movie stars walking down the red carpet to be photographed, the fashion luminaries of that time were photographed and written about, and some included what they were wearing. These pages show the important names of that time attending the event—Diana Vreeland, Bill Blass, Perry Ellis, Gerry Stutz, Oscar and Francoise de la Renta, Pierre Bergé, Ron Shamask, Donna Karan, Ralph Lauren, Calvin Klein, Marina Schiano, Mary McFadden, and Fernando Sanchez.

Louise faces the

Diana Vreeland and Bill Blass

Gerry Stutz

CeCe and Barry Kieselstein-Cord

Parry Ellis and Lynn Kohlman

Pierre Berge

Mollie Parnis and Cathy di Montezemolo

Oscar and Francoise de la Renta

Kal Ruttenstein

Dawn Mello

Joe Brooks

Ira and Jackie Neimark

Ron Shamask

Donna Karan

NEW YORK — As I watched the shining limousines lumbering through the snow Thursday night (oh, the chic ol black on white!), I realized the fashion flakes were going to brave that "Dr. Zhivago" blizzard after all. It was the dinner at the New York Public Library for those very controversial Council of Fashion Designers of America Awards, and I was expecting fashion friction. But somehow the fiery confrontations over that misbegotten award last summer seemed so long ago. Tempers had cooled with the temperatures, and nearly all of my designing darlings were there to show a rare spirit of family community.

Intrepid souls! One after another, with umbrellas and evening shoes in hand, trying to maintain some semblance of their distinctive styles as they took that endless trek past the stone lions through that stormy white night: Diana Vreeland, in Givenchy stepping high like a racehorse, flanked by so-suave Bill Blass and his even more dapper chauffeur; CeCe Kieselstein-Cord, hiking up the skirts of her black Galanos very provocative heights (perhaps in homage to our lady of the legs, Slim Keith); mix-and-match Arnold Scaasi, with a red and black umbrella to match his red and black tie and car; and international Oscar de la Renta, with his Bermuda rental umbrella, and wife Francoise riding with ty Pierre Berge for the evening in rubber boots who said she felt just like a bag lady.

Once inside, everyone was welcome by Sergeant-Major Mary McFadden, who had the evening very efficiently in hand, right down to the McFadden "Crystal Dream" bedsheets used as tablecloths for Glorious Foods' dinner spread and the gilded squash and cranberry centerpieces. Major Mary explained that only the legal husbands and wives of the CFDA members

Even a blizzard did not stop a flurry of top designers and fashion industry leaders from attending the Council of Fashion Designers of America Awards at the New York Public Library, and the legendary fashion writer Louise J. Esterhazy was there to cover it all in "Louise Faces the Fashion Flakes," Women's Wear Daily, Monday, January 18, 1982.

ashion flakes

Vreeland and Blass

Ralph Lauren

The new elegant Calvin Klein and Marina Schiano

WWD photos
by LAURIE SAGALYN

Major McFadden and Fernando Sanchez

Robert Lighton

Separate tables

were allowed in on the same ticket. "They wouldn't bring anyone if not related by marriage," said Military Mary. "So we're quite heavy on the men, to say the least."

So it was fortunate for a fashion-watcher like myself that those merry men showed more diversity in their black-tie get-ups than usual: British Khaki's Robert Lighton in a khaki dinner jacket, of course, to match Perry Ellis' pants; glittering Lee Brooks, of Alex and Lee, who wore one of his own gem-studded neck pieces in lieu of a tie (I myself wore a tie instead of a necklace); the Bishop of Bloomingdale's, Kal Ruttenstein, who scandalously appeared without his high mass vestments (One more time, Kal, and you'll be defrocked) and Geoffrey Beene, who wore his "Invisible Man" suit.

I thought the 1982 model of the new elegant Calvin Klein looked smashing, especially standing next to fashion diva Marina Schiano, draped in slinky YSL. Elegant Calvin was describing his new Central Park West apartment. "Upstairs, it's just like Connecticut," said rustic Cal, "especially when you open the windows and look out on the snow in the park. But I do keep hearing strange noises, all alone in this new place." "Oh, poor darling, all alone, eh?" purred insinuating Marina.

Oh, by the way, there were some awards given, though I'd had entirely too much champagne by that time to really recall what or to whom. I did notice Major McFadden carefully applying lipstick (and when she should have been applauding), just before she stepped up to the podium, and the fact that Bella Donna Karan took her reading glasses off halfway through her speech. But when I learned that I myself was not receiving an award, I left in a huff.

— LOUISE J. ESTERHAZY

CLOCKWISE FROM TOP LEFT: *Diana Vreeland and Bill Blass; CeCe and Barry Kieselstein-Cord; Perry Ellis and Lynn Kohlman; Pierre Berge; Diana Vreeland and Bill Blass; Ralph Lauren; Calvin Klein and Marina Schiano; Robert Lighton; Major McFadden and Fernando Sanchez; Mollie Parnis and Cathy di Montezemolo; Dawn Mello and Joe Brooks; Kal Ruttenstein; Oscar and Francoise de la Renta; Donna Karan; Ron Shamask; Ira and Jackie Neimark; and Geraldine Stutz. (Reprinted courtesy of* Women's Wear Daily.*)*

More Fashionable Events

BOTH OF NEW YORK'S FAMOUS fashion schools, FIT and Parsons School of Design, have a tradition of holding annual awards ceremonies. There are two purposes, both important: the first is to raise funds for scholarships; the second, to raise their profile and their fashion reputation.

In 1976, Calvin Klein was quoted as saying, "It was a coup for us to get Betty Ford as the guest of honor" at the Parsons event. The honored guest designers were a who's who in the fashion industry of the time. They included Liz Claiborne, Shannon Rogers, Calvin Klein, Donna Karan, Donald Brooks, Kasper, Kay Unger, and Chester Weinberg. A good example of the many FIT awards dinners honored Arthur Ochs Sulzberger, at which nearly 1,000 guests crowded into an elegant dinner at the Waldorf Astoria.

In 1985, I was selected by Parsons to be the guest of honor at the Parsons Fashion Critic Awards Dinner. Here too are photos of some of the high-profile fashion luminaries at that elegant affair—among them, Stephen Weiss and Donna Karan, Carolyne Roehm, Michael Kors, and Isaac Mizrahi.

Betty Ford (front and center) with guests including Liz Claiborne, Shannon Rogers, Leo Narducci, Anthony Muto, Calvin Klein, Piero Dimitri, Ann Keagy, Donna Karan, Donald Brooks, Albert Capraro, Kasper, Kay Unger, and Chester Weinberg at a 1976 event at Parsons. (Photo courtesy of Ira Neimark.)

LESSON LEARNED

As everyone undoubtedly knows, for any social event, charitable or otherwise, it is necessary to not only feature important business and social names as guests or sponsors but also to include high-profile fashion designers and theatrical stars. This is a proven formula that successfully demonstrated who is in the front row of any and all fashion events.

FROM TOP, LEFT TO RIGHT: *Ira Neimark, Bill Arnold, and Polly Bergen; Orlanda Olsen (center); Laura and John Pomerantz; Pat Forrest and Jack Mulqueen; Muffy and Norman Wechsler; and Jackie and Ira Neimark. (Photos by Pierre Scherman courtesy of* Women's Wear Daily.*)*

FROM TOP, LEFT TO RIGHT: *Bernie Goodman and Pauline Trigère.* *(Photo by Pierre Scherman courtesy of* Women's Wear Daily.*) Ira Neimark; Laura Mardirossian and Bill Blass; Rose Wells and Joe Brooks. (Photos by Nick Machalaba courtesy of* Women's Wear Daily.*)*

The fashion press was there to cover Philip M. Hawley, then chairman of Carter Hawley Hale Stores, Inc., introduce me as the honoree before a crowd of nearly 1,100 retailers and manufacturers at the Waldorf-Astoria for a dinner that benefited the National Jewish Hospital. As the Thursday, May 9, 1985 Women's Wear Daily article, "Neimark's Night," reported, "the award [meant] a great deal to [me] because 42 years ago [I] had stood in the same room watching [my] 'hero' and mentor, Bonwit Teller president William M. Holmes, receive the same award. . . .With a bit of self-deprecating humor, [I] mused, 'forty-two years is a long time. I wonder what took me so long?'" (Reprinted courtesy of Women's Wear Daily.)

WOMEN'S WEAR DAILY, THURSDAY, APRIL 21, 1988

EYEVIEW

PARSONS' NIGHT OF TALENT AND PASSION

Ira Neimark talked about "talent and passion" in New York Tuesday night and said he was seeing a lot of it, as the students of Parsons School of Design put their fashions on the runway. The Bergdorf Goodman chairman himself was in the spotlight as the guest of honor at the Parsons Fashion Critic Awards Dinner at the Marriott Marquis Hotel.

The retailer told the crowd his dream was to create the best specialty store in New York, "if not America," and he thanked those that helped him do it — including his wife, **Jackie, Dawn Mello,** Bergdorf's president, and **Steve Elkin,** the vice chairman.

The evening attracted some 1,300 guests and raised about $500,000 for the school's scholarship fund. **Donna Karan** made history as both the first female and the first graduate to chair the event in its 22-year history. Karan, as well as Mello, gave the nod to evening pants for the black-tie evening.

In the crowd, **Linda Wachner** took down names for possible future Warnaco staff and said the costume parade finale, with the theme "A Weekend with Napoleon" and tutored, as usual, by **Donald Brooks,** was the most fun. Gary Markle, of London, Ontario, the Student Designer of the Year, noted he has already been interviewing — with **Charlotte Neuville** and **Adrienne Vittadini** — but added his first choice would be to work with **Issey Miyake,** then **Kenzo.** Clean-shaven Markle had reluctantly removed his **Don Johnson** beard for the show. "I promised **Frank Rizzo** [chairman of the Parsons Fashion Department] I would," Markle said.

Bob Mackie was impressed with the "sportswear." He will not only direct the costume portion of the Otis Art Institute of Parsons Awards in Los Angeles next week — the theme is "Cinderella in the Sixties" — but also he will be its honoree.

Getting one of the biggest reactions on the runway was student designer **Carlos Urrutia's** black pailletted slipdress with a large New York subway token embroidered on the derriere. It will become part of the permanent collection of the Museum of the City of New York. Joanne Olian, curator of costumes, plans to pick a dress every year from now on that captures the spirit of New York.

A look from "A Weekend with Napoleon"

Carlos Urrutia's subway token dress

John and Laura Pomerantz

Ira and Jackie Neimark

Student Designer of the Year Gary Markle and his award-winning dress

Nina Santisi and Isaac Mizrahi

Carmelo Pomodoro

Kitty D'Alessio

Stephan Weiss and Donna Karan

Lawrence Wechsler

Patrick Kelly

Gold Thimble winner Claudia Acavedo and Carolyne Roehm

Andrew Rosen and Jack Mulqueen

Michael Kors

Ellin Saltzman

William Ruben; Gerald Shaw

Linda Wachner

Mohan Murjani

Jack Shultz

Louis Dell'Olio

Tomio and Beverly Ann Taki

"A Weekend with Napoleon" was the theme for a Parsons School of Design's Fashion Critics Awards Dinner at the Marriot Marquis hotel that raised $500,000 for the school's scholarship fund. According to the Thursday, April 21, 1988 Women's Wear Daily article, "Parsons' Night of Talent and Passion," Donna Karan "made history as both the first female and the first graduate to chair the event in its 22-year history." Guests included Bob Mackie, Michael Kors, and Isaac Mizrahi, as well as other leading designers of the day and top industry leaders. I was again in the spotlight as guest of honor. (Reprinted courtesy of Women's Wear Daily.)

DAILY NEWS RECORD, THURSDAY, APRIL 21, 1988

BETWEEN THE LINES

EDITED BY TIMOTHY HAWKINS

CAN IVANA BE FAR BEHIND? BTL's favorite piece of mail of the week . . . or should we say month . . . oh! let's go for the year, was the "media alert" from a store's public relations department headlined "Blaine Trump to Visit Macy's." This all happened Wednesday at the Herald Square flagship. So what, you ask? So she could see the Movado watch collection in the fine jewelry department. So what, you ask? Well, ABT dancers were autographing souvenir programs and Blaine was chairperson of the gala premiere of the company's production of "Gaite Parisienne" that night, with much ballyhooed costumes by CHRISTIAN LACROIX. So what, you ask? Don't ask us, ask Macy's.

Manhattan's Nick and Pat di Paolo

Ira Neimark table hops at Parsons

Parsons' Gary Lisz

Stephen Kaplan

Michael O'Donnell's ensemble

Bradley Erickson's designs

Student chic

Linda Wachner

PARSONS HONORS IRA: "Wow!" was the first thing out of IRA NEIMARK's mouth when he took the stage at the Marriott Marquis to receive the Parsons Award at the design school's annual Fashion Critics Awards Show and dinner. It was a pretty Wowie group of designers and industry power houses, as well, that turned out to honor Bergdorf Goodman's chairman and CEO and, hopefully, to be wowed by the show of student fashions. After quoting Thoreau, Neimark told the dressed-to-the-nines crowd in the room and the students, who dined in the balcony area above, that he knew only two things necessary to make it in the fashion biz — talent and a passion to succeed. Then he told the graduating seniors to "follow your dreams." The student designs that followed were, thankfully, not nightmarish. But neither were they as dreamy as they have been in past shows. Instead, most took a safe route — not surprising when you consider last week's fall collections from New York designers, who seemed to be organizing a safety patrol on Seventh Avenue. Winners in Parsons' men's wear categories included MICHAEL O'DONNELL, who received the Jeffrey Banks Gold Thimble Award, and BRADLEY ERICKSON, who garnered Bill Robinson's Gold Thimble.

PHOTOS BY TIMOTHY HAWKINS

Judge Jeff Banks

Cecilia Metheny, Fred Henry

At Parson School of Design's Fashion Critics Awards show and dinner fundraiser for the school's scholarship fund, "Neimark told the dressed-to-the-nines crowd in the room and the students, who dined in the balcony area above, that he knew only two things necessary to make it in the fashion biz—talent and a passion to succeed," reported Daily News Record's *Thursday, April 21, 1988 coverage of the event. (Reprinted courtesy of* Daily News Record.)

Jacqueline de Ribes and Joanne Herring. (Photo courtesy Women's Wear Daily.*)*

Geoffrey Beene:
It Was Great to Know You

IN MARCH 1985 Prince Schwarzenberg of Austria held a dinner party in honor of Geoffrey Beene. The dinner took place at the Palais Schwarzenberg in Vienna. Helen Von Damm was the U.S. ambassador to Austria at that time and remained a great friend to Geoffrey for many years. My wife, Jackie, and I sat at Geoffrey's table with Helen O'Hagan, a top executive at Saks Fifth Avenue; Dawn Mello, president of Bergdorf Goodman; and Bernadine Morris, the feature fashion editor for *The New York Times*.

The event marked one of several U.S. embassy presentations in Europe that Geoffrey enjoyed in the late seventies through the eighties. My wife and I were fortunate to attend many of Geoffrey's fashion shows in the palaces and American embassies in the capital cities of Europe.

Looking at a photograph of that memorable evening brings back great memories. It takes me "fast back" to 1946, when I first met Geoffrey. I had just returned from the war in the Pacific to rejoin Bonwit Teller, as the assistant merchandise control manager. Bonwit Teller also employed Henry Ginsberg, a friend of Geoffrey's, in the bookkeeping department. One day, soon after, Henry invited me to meet Geoffrey. Geoffrey was from Louisiana, Henry from

Dinner in Vienna (clockwise from left): *Jackie Neimark, Bernadine Morris, Geoffrey Beene, Helen O'Hagan, Dawn Mello, and Ira Neimark. (Photo courtesy of* Women's Wear Daily.)

Mississippi, and I had to listen carefully to understand their Southern accents. It did not, in any case, take them too long to sound like sophisticated New Yorkers. Geoffrey, at that time, was a draper for Teal Traina, a top American fashion designer. He had tremendous talent, which eventually brought him to leadership in not only American fashion designers but European as well.

I recall a few experiences that have nothing to do with fashion design. Around 1947 or 1948, Geoffrey and Henry were in a taxicab accident in New York City. The insurance settlement afforded them a trip to Paris. This may or may not have been Geoffrey's first trip to Europe, but it was the one he always remembered.

I followed Geoffrey's career over the years when I worked in New England. His success as one of the top fashion designers in America and in Europe was no surprise to me, knowing his early ambition. When I arrived at Bergdorf Goodman to become the CEO in 1975, I had the opportunity to open an exclusive Geoffrey Beene shop on the second floor, overlooking the Plaza. A fitting business tribute to two ambitious young men who met many years ago.

LESSONS LEARNED

Observe the talented, ambitious people around you. There is often a future star out there waiting to be discovered. It might be you.

Enjoy good friendships. They don't last forever.

Diana, The Princess

WHENEVER I AM ASKED to speak at university business schools, business groups, and even schools for underprivileged children, the Princess Diana stories always receive the greatest attention and enjoyment. At the risk of repeating myself in my first book, *Crossing Fifth Avenue to Bergdorf Goodman*, I will again tell the stories as I recall them.

My wife, Jackie, and I were very fortunate to take our many trips to Europe required by the retailers for whom I worked during the sixties through the eighties. They started in the sixties with G. Fox & Co., carried into the early seventies for B. Altman, and for Bergdorf Goodman in the mid-seventies up to the early nineties. All in all, for more than 25 years, we traveled to Europe possibly more than 50 times. With all this traveling, one trip stands out more than any other. It was the trip when we met Princess Diana for the first time.

Whenever my European trips took me to Milan and then to Paris, the week in between the fashion shows in those two cities allowed time to visit London. The prime purpose for my London visit was to maintain Bergdorf Goodman's relationship with Turnbull & Asser, the world-famous men's haberdasher. The second was to attend the British Fashion Guild's designer fashion presentations. Other courtesy visits were made to Eddie Rayne of Delman's, Bergdorf's long-time women's shoe lease, and to Sheila Pickles (a great name), the head of the perfumer Penhaligon's of London.

Unfortunately, the British fashion designers, except for a few forward-thinking designers, were not quite up to Paris or Milan. However, the British Fashion Guild, possibly aware of this shortcoming, devised a social schedule not to be missed. Each season, spring and fall, a reception was held for visiting retailers. One season, a reception was held to meet British royalty at a wonderfully famous palace, the next season to meet the prime minister at 10 Downing Street.

Needless to say, most, if not all, the retailers showed up. My wife's and my first invitation was for us to be introduced to Princess Diana. With that invitation in hand, I telephoned Ken Williams, the manager of Turnbull & Asser on Jermyn Street. I told Ken of our invitation to meet the princess. My question was, since Ken was well connected to the Prince and Princess of Wales, would it be proper for me to wear a navy-and-red rep tie with a white button-down shirt? I can still recall hearing Ken's voice, loud and clear over the phone. "No, no, that will never do," he instructed in his impeccable English accent.

He then said that he would "run up" a tie for me to wear, in teal blue, the princess's favorite color for her husband, and a white-on-white shirt, to complete the proper appearance. Further, he would have the ensemble delivered to my hotel the next day in time for the princess's reception. All this with one caveat: "Don't tell anyone about the next-day delivery since Turnbull's normal delivery for a special order is two weeks." I kept my promise of silence for Turnbull & Asser's special delivery for many, many years.

Princess Diana at the Metropolitan Museum of Art's Costume Institute gala, 1996. (Photo by Steve Eichner courtesy of Women's Wear Daily.*)*

The reception at the Fishmongers' Hall (a strange name for one of the most magnificent palaces in London) was a royal strategy. There were two reception rooms. One was small, allowing about 20 high-level guests to be personally introduced to Princess Diana. The other was quite large with about 200 guests.

While waiting in the smaller room, one by one, the six princess's ladies-in-waiting came down a small staircase, one more beautiful than the last. Finally, the princess, a young woman of movie-star-quality appearance and demeanor, came down the staircase. She held a small bouquet of violets.

Eddie Rayne (soon to be Sir Edward) positioned Jackie and me first in line to meet Princess Diana. When Eddie introduced me as the chairman and CEO of Bergdorf Goodman, I felt the normal greeting "How pleased I am to meet you" would not do for what I went through to properly dress for the occasion. I said, "Your Royal Highness, I am very pleased to meet you. In your honor, Ken Williams ran this tie up for me to wear to your reception," to which the princess replied, "Mr. Neimark, the blue tie matches your eyes."

This statement has and will live with me for many years to come.

To cap the introduction off, when meeting my wife, the princess asked, "And what do you do while your husband is busy all day?" to which Jackie replied, "He promised to take me to Jack Barkley's to buy me a Jaguar."

"How wonderful, I have a Jaguar," said the princess, who then moved on to meet the other 20 or so guests while Jackie and I stood there mesmerized.

Following this small reception, the princess went into the large room to greet the 200 or so guests. Later, we learned that the small bouquet of violets the princess carried made it possible for her not to have to shake hands with so many more people throughout this large reception that followed our more intimate meeting.

There are a number of sequels to go with this story that will be covered in other chapters.

LESSON LEARNED

Whenever the opportunity presents itself to meet not only royalty but also other high-profile celebrities and business executives, it is important to wear the proper clothes and make an appropriate greeting in order to make a lasting favorable impression.

EXPERIENCES LEARNED ALONG THE WAY

Experiences with the Fashion Press

MY RELATIONSHIPS with the fashion press began with a shocker. In 1970 James Brady, the former publisher of *Woman's Wear Daily*, sent a reporter to interview Randy Stambaugh, the president of B. Altman & Co. He asked, "Now that Best & Company is closing, when will that happen to B. Altman?" Randy Stambaugh, handsome and always the perfect gentleman, reminded me of a character out of an F. Scott Fitzgerald novel. He may well have come close to losing his cool or temper but said nothing more than "This interview is over." The following day the story came out with the headline "Stambaugh Takes the Fifth on Fifth." Possibly a great headline, but I considered it a distortion and dirty pool.

From that day forward, I was always acutely aware and sensitive about what I said whenever I spoke to a newspaper reporter, fashion or otherwise. I was as careful as if I were skating on thin ice, because with the press, I felt I was. Early on I recognized the importance of developing business relationships (networking) with executives in all phases of retailing from fashion designers to wholesalers. Finally when I reached the position that brought me to the attention of the press, representing B. Altman and then Bergdorf Goodman, I saw a significant distinction between retail executives and the press. The executives were either buying or selling merchandise. This was familiar to me. The press, however, was publishing and that was all new to me.

I also realized two important facts: First, the press offered great opportunity to advance my business objectives, and second, if not handled properly, my efforts would be fraught with peril.

The emergence of the fashion press, an extraordinary group of creative fashion reporters, developed to fine art concurrently with the rise of the French fashion designers during the seventies through the nineties. From the beginning, Eugenia Sheppard wrote wonderful stories in the *International Herald Tribune* about my efforts to bring the French couture to Bergdorf Goodman. Eugenia's stories were followed by those of Hebe Dorsey, then Suzy Menkes; Etta Froio at *Women's Wear Daily*; and Bernadine Morris at *The New York Times*. All these talented fashion writers enormously helped highlight the reemergence of Bergdorf Goodman.

LESSON LEARNED

Whatever the type of business, the financial press, fashion press, entertainment press, and so on are always looking for new products as well as new concepts and new ideas to interest and to stimulate their readers. It is critical to recognize which reporter at which publication is sympathetic, supportive, and very interested in your business concept or model.

Fashion Writers and
Bergdorf Goodman

A VERY IMPORTANT FASHION WRITER who enormously helped advance the cause of Bergdorf Goodman's emergence was Bernadine Morris of *The New York Times*. One of her first stories about Bergdorf Goodman was published on January 26, 1978, while she covered the French couture shows in Paris. She had a paragraph in her couture story about my efforts in Paris that brought a great amount of attention to the people in the fashion business in the United States and abroad. The paragraph read as follows:

> One of Givenchy's admirers is Bergdorf Goodman's
> Ira Neimark, the only American store president
> currently buying couture clothes. He is carrying
> around a portfolio of almost life-size drawings of new
> shops on the store's second floor, which will house
> Saint Laurent, Givenchy and the Dior collections.
> The shops will include both couture and ready-to-
> wear styles, which is an innovation the designers
> appreciate. They haven't figured out a way to do it
> themselves.

"It Was Just a Little Dinner Party at Versailles," The New York Times, *Sunday, July 30, 1978. Grace Mirabella, Louise Rouet, Philippe Venet, Nan Kempner, Lynn Wyatt, Hubert Givenchy, Gerald Van der Kemp, Jackie Neimark, Estée Lauder, and Tatiana Liberman. (Photos © The New York Times.)*

Another highlight from Bernadine ran in the *Times* Style section in July 1978. In this story, she covered the dinner party given by the curator Gerald Van der Kemp. The party was held in my honor for reintroducing French couture to the United States and for donating the proceeds of the Bergdorf Goodman couture fashion show to the restoration of Giverny, the impressionist painter Claude Monet's home and gardens. *The New York Times* featured a great picture of my wife, Jackie, wearing an American gown designed by Mary McFadden. The entire event was an experience beyond my comprehension.

Amid Hapsburg Splendor, a Gala at the Met

By BERNADINE MORRIS

Martha Graham with Halston, above; Pat Buckley, left, Mary Sykes Cahan, in black strapless dresses by Bill Blass, below.

Jacqueline Onassis, Hugh Fraser and Kurt Waldheim at exhibition; left, Empress Elizabeth's organdie dress.

"Amid Hapsburg Splendor, a Gala at the Met," The New York Times, *Tuesday, December 4, 1979. The exhibition was organized by Diana Vreeland and shows Martha Graham and Halston; Pat Buckley and Mary Sykes Cahan; an organdy dress worn by Empress Elizabeth of Austria; Jacqueline Onassis, Hugh Fraser, and Kurt Waldheim* (clockwise from top left). *(Photos © The New York Times.)*

Another great Bernadine story, "Hapsburg Splendor, a Gala at the Met," ran on December 4, 1979. As she had done before, Bernadine mentioned my wife, Jackie, this time wearing a Stavropoulos gown from Bergdorf Goodman.

Suzy Menkes, another great fashion writer of the *International Herald Tribune*, wrote in March of 1989, "Bernadine Morris, fashion editor of *The New York Times*, and Ira Neimark, chairman of Bergdorf Goodman, have been made chevaliers of the Legion of Honor by French Culture Minister Jack Lang." It would seem the French and the Italians, unlike the Americans, took great pride in their couture.

Another fashion writer who helped raise the profile of Bergdorf Goodman was Hebe Dorsey of the *International Herald Tribune*, who replaced Eugenia Sheppard when Eugenia retired. Hebe wrote many interesting stories about Bergdorf Goodman's efforts to reach its lofty objectives in the world of luxury fashion, but one article, "London: Elegance Is In," in the *Tribune*, October 11, 1986, tells it all. I note one paragraph:

> Radiant in a Bruce Oldfield off-the-shoulder, royal purple velvet dress, Princess Diana had seated on her left the minister of state for industry, Giles Shaw, and seated on her right, Ira Neimark, chairman of Bergdorf Goodman.

Enough said!

LESSON LEARNED
It is important to never forget the press can make you or break you. The press can do you and your business a lot of good, if they are treated as partners in your endeavors. If treated otherwise, you do so at your own peril.

Accomplishments and Recognition

Each of the merchandising strategies and business programs implemented from the beginning brought about sales and profit results far beyond what most anyone thought possible, particularly our competition. To accomplish our objective to become the leading fashion retailer in New York, we developed the following strategies for success:

- Aggressive marketing of European and American fashion designers.
- Inventory management via unit weeks of supply.
- Vendor programs—agreed-to growth and profit strategies with each and every fashion designer house and supplier.
- An extremely knowledgeable and professional fashion office with direct oversight on all buying decisions in order to create a Bergdorf Goodman fashion point of view.
- A highly talented buying and merchandising staff.
- A financial division dedicated to financial discipline and inventory management—with a merchant's point of view and not bean counters.

- A public relations office to coordinate all merchandising objectives in order to create a highly recognizable profile of fashion leadership.
- Display talent with an understanding of what environment the sophisticated fashion customer feels comfortable with and wants to see and to be surrounded by
- A personnel department to recruit talented salespeople who must have an understanding of our fashion objectives and ability to relate to fashion-conscious customers. (Salespeople were instructed to dress reflecting the store image, not their own.)
- A creative advertising department reporting to me (a long-ago ambition of mine realized!).

These strategies and business practices may look like a résumé to be presented to a potential employer, and that is not far from the mark. We felt, if we had the fashion designers on our side, the proper salespeople in place, and assortments equal to or larger than our competition, the customers (our employers) would come. And did they ever.

Women's Wear Daily, recognizing our accomplishments and rewarding Bergdorf Goodman with a two-page spread, wrote the following:

> Bergdorf Goodman's advantage point by the Plaza Hotel on Fifth Avenue has always given it a special cachet, but now, as its interior is being cultivated into jewel perfection, Bergdorf's is giving the term "specialty store" a new meaning.

LESSONS LEARNED

Whatever the task, it is most important to have a vision and a direction for all involved to enthusiastically understand, accept, and support that vision.

Those employed to help accomplish the objectives but lack understanding of the vision should be released to work for the competition.

The Goddess in the Fountain

M ANY YEARS AGO, around the turn of the nineteenth century, on the corner of Fifth Avenue and 58th Street, stood the magnificent Vanderbilt mansion. Before it stood the beautiful Pulitzer Fountain with the statue of Pomona.

As time marched on, in the mid-twenties, the Vanderbilt mansion came down and was replaced by another magnificent building—Bergdorf Goodman. People often ask if Bergdorf

Vanderbilt mansion, Pulitzer Fountain. (Photo courtesy of Ira Neimark.)

Pulitzer Fountain, Grand Army Plaza (Photo courtesy of Ira Neimark.)

Goodman is the original mansion. It is so beautiful. The answer, of course, is no. But we felt responsible to maintain the standard of elegance and luxury deserved for that location.

As with any piece of art, time and weather will take its toll. Unfortunately, the bronze Pomona, goddess of tree fruit, and her fountain was no exception. When I arrived at Bergdorf Goodman, the fountain worked in fits and starts, and was eventually shut down. Until, like in fables, knights in shining armor appeared, bringing Pomona and her fountain back to life, as noted in a *New York Times* article dated October 24, 1988:

> In 1988, Leonard Lauder, then president and chief executive officer of Estée Lauder, formed a group, the Grand Army Plaza Partnership. The private partnership is also led by Ira Neimark, chairman and chief executive officer of Bergdorf Goodman, and Ira Millstein, senior partner of Weil, Gotshal & Manges, which has offices in the GM Building.

Needless to say, the necessary funds were raised to bring Pomona and her fountain back to her former glory, for all to enjoy.

LESSONS LEARNED

When a city administration has so many different priorities and constituents to satisfy, many areas of beauty can be neglected.

As represented here, private (business) donors set a standard for others to follow.

P.S. Unfortunately, the magnificent bronze plaque and chain commemorating the event were stolen within a few days of the restoration ceremony. Which brings to mind "No good deed goes unpunished."

Geoffrey Beene and
the Guerlain Shop

BUILDING AND FEATURING different fashion designer shops during the period of developing Bergdorf Goodman to its full potential occurred in a number of different ways. Most of the shops were designer-inspired. As an example, early on, when we told Geoffrey Beene that we would like to have his shop, exclusive with Bergdorf Goodman, on the second floor (replacing Halston), he agreed, only with the provision that he would personally design his own shop.

Having Geoffrey Beene, one of the most creative fashion designers of the day, use his talents to design his shop or boutique for us was a big plus. Allowing the creative geniuses of the day to help to create the "Bergdorf image" went a long way to achieving our objective. This "designer–shop approach" with fashion designers became a fine art of negotiation. Each designer, in turn, receiving recognition from the fashion press and fashion-conscious customers, felt strongly that he or she had earned his or her location and look in Bergdorf Goodman.

Another very dramatic and successful example of this approach happened in Paris in the spring of 1982 when Dawn Mello told me she had something to show me. We drove to the Champs-Élysées. When the car pulled to the curb, Dawn asked me to close

Bergdorf's makes room for Guerlain shop

NEW YORK — Ira Neimark, chairman and chief executive officer of Bergdorf Goodman, will strike another blow for exclusivity in early April when he opens a Guerlain shop on the store's first floor. According to Neimark and Michel Vincent, president of Guerlain, Inc., Bergdorf's will be the only store with a Guerlain shop, and the only one to carry Guerlain's Issima skin care line, now sold only in the international market.

The Guerlain Boutique, to be called Guerlain at Bergdorf's, is the centerpiece of a renovation and expansion of the store's cosmetics department. By next spring, when construction is completed, cosmetics space will be increased 50 percent, with total cosmetics volume expected to increase by a similar amount, one industry source said. More lines, as yet undetermined, will be added, the presentation of other lines will be improved and treatment rooms will be built, Neimark said. The expansion is part of a step-by-step overhaul of the entire store.

Guerlain at Bergdorf's will be in the oval rotunda in front of three elevators facing the 58th

> "It's recognition of the effort they are making to look different, to be different."
> — Michel Vincent

Street entrance. The space is now occupied by fragrances, which will move to the area now housing the Hermes boutique. That shop will move out of the store in early spring, according to Dawn Mello, president.

Cosmetics will also be expanded into the area adjacent to the Hermes boutique not now used for selling.

Neimark said fixturing and decor of the new areas will be "dramatic-within the taste level of Bergdorf Goodman." Construction in the fragrance area of a miniature version of the fountain outside the Plaza Hotel is being considered. One source estimated the first-floor renovation would cost one-fifth of the amount being spent on the entire store renovation, a figure Neimark placed at $15 million.

The 400-square-foot Guerlain shop will be modeled on the Guerlain shop on the Champs d'Ely-

> "We're first going to make a success of the venture with Bergdorf Goodman before thinking of rolling."
> — Vincent

sees, one of four Guerlain shops in Paris. It will contain four marble counters, one in each corner of the rotunda. Although details have not been completely worked out, Vincent said at least two of the counters will be used for the treatment line, with the remainder of the space devoted to fragrances. The center of the floor, which now holds a fragrance bar, will be empty, Mello said. The boutique will quadruple Guerlain's space at the store. Although Neimark declined to comment on his projections for sales at the boutique, one source said they are expected to exceed $1,000 per square foot.

According to Vincent, discussions between Guerlain and Bergdorf's have been going on for about two years. Bergdorf's was an appropriate choice for the boutique because Neimark's concern with obtaining exclusive merchandise corresponds to Guerlain's objective to stay at the extreme upper end of the market, Vincent said. "It's recognition of the effort they are making to look different, to be different," he said.

Some of the most recent examples of Neimark's quest for exclusivity are the construction of the Musee des Arts Decoratifs home furnishings shop, which opened Oct. 26, and an Angela Cummings jewelry shop, planned for next year. Neimark also demonstrated that concern in June when Bergdorf's said it would no longer carry Halston ready-to-wear and cosmetics after the designer signed a licensing deal with J.C. Penney for the Halston III apparel line.

Vincent and Neimark said the contract between Bergdorf's and Guerlain does not set a time limit for the exclusivity. They would not discuss the financial stipulations of the contract. Vincent declined to predict when the treatment line would be expanded to other stores. "We're first going to make a success of the venture with Bergdorf Goodman before thinking of rolling out," Vincent said.

Issima is the best-selling of three Guerlain treatment lines, none of which have ever been sold here. It accounts for about 20 percent of Guerlain's worldwide treatment volume. Its 12 stockkeeping units include four foundations, day and night creams, eye and neck creams, a body cream, ampoules, a mask and a cleanser. Prices have not been firmly set, but will probably range from about

A sketch of the planned Guerlain shop at Bergdorf Goodman

$37.50 for the foundation to $95 for the ampoules.

The products are aimed at women over 30, and are based on an ingredient called Hydrolastine, a combination of elastine, silicon collagen and lactic acid. They were developed by Guerlain's research lab in Chartres and were launched in Europe in 1989.

"It's a direct attack on La Prairie," Vincent said, referring to Jacqueline Cochran's high-price, narrowly distributed treatment line.

Promotional plans for the line have not been completed, but will include heavy sampling, said Nick Jordan, Guerlain's vice president of sales. There will be skin care clinics, either in groups or on a one-to-one basis, and counter consultants will keep a card on each customer. Jordan believes the line has the potential for a large mail order business at Bergdorf's.

The Guerlain shop will also exclusively sell several fragrances now sold only in Europe — Vol de Nuit, Eau Cologne du Coq, Eau de Fleurs de Cedrat, Eau de Guerlain and Apres L'Ondee. There will also be line extensions in the Jicky fragrance line.

— NORMA SEXTON

Ira Neimark (above), Guerlain's Issima eye cream, Michel Vincent (below)

Ira Neimark and Michael Vincent. (Photo © The New York Times.)

my eyes, while she directed me across the sidewalk into a shop that had a wonderful fragrance. I opened my eyes and exclaimed, "This shop looks just like the inside of the 58th Street entrance to Bergdorf Goodman." The wonderful shop was Guerlain at 68 des Champs-Élysées. Dawn and her staff found another winner.

As I mentioned earlier, our strategy was for Dawn to identify the winners and I was to convince the fashion company how they would fit into our Bergdorf Goodman merchandising strategy.

I introduced myself to Jean-Pierre Guerlain, the chief executive of Guerlain. He was the personification of the image that I had in my mind of French aristocracy, the ultimate gentleman in every way. My proposal of duplicating his Champs-Élyseés Guerlain shop exclusively in Bergdorf Goodman's 58th Street alcove intrigued him. I was able to convince him that this would be the perfect manner to introduce Guerlain perfumes to the American market. (The Lauder family used this same strategy, having Bergdorf Goodman introduce Origins nearly 10 years later.)

My next stop was to meet Jean-Paul Guerlain, "the Nose." A key member of any and all perfumers was and is the nose, an expert with the talent of having the expertise of developing new fragrances. Jean-Paul Guerlain created such perfumes as Samsara. I guess I passed muster, since shortly after my meetings with the Guerlain family, the first Guerlain boutique in America opened at Bergdorf Goodman. It was a duplicate of the gem on the Champs-Élysées.

LESSONS LEARNED

It is important to be guided by a professional with a concept that fits into your vision and strategy. In order to have the project come to a successful conclusion, it is best to go to the head of the organization involved.

The expression "Never talk to angels when you can talk to God" has always made sense to me and has brought about many more successes than failures.

The Nose of the Beholder

IN 1985, DAWN, fellow Bergdorf executive Steve Elkin, and I agreed it would be to our advantage to have a Bergdorf Goodman perfume, a fragrance exclusively Bergdorf's. Each influenced within our own sphere—Dawn's from a fashion point of view, Steve's from a financial one, and mine from management—we felt we could make it profitable. From a merchandising and image point of view, it fit into my overall strategy.

We went through all the steps, retaining fragrance specialists, bottle design people, perfume research consultants, and other experts. We even went to the extreme, taking a consulting room in the Plaza Hotel in order not to have everyday business interfere with our deliberations. When we were far enough along, we felt it only right and politically correct to tell the executives at the home office, Carter Hawley Hale, about our plans and brought a sample of what we had at that point.

After we reviewed our figures and the progress we were making as we normally did, at our quarterly meeting at the CHH headquarters in Los Angeles, we told them about our BG perfume project. Attending the meeting, in addition to Dawn, Steve, and myself, were about five key CHH executives: the CEO, president, treasurer, operations, and a controller.

Dawn passed the very fancy perfume bottle around the conference table, and each in turn took the top off the bottle to smell the sample. As each took his or her turn and inhaled, each made a comment; most went something like "very mild" or "a good aroma" or "a very pleasant fragrance," and so on.

Finally the controller, a very bookish person whom we were not familiar with, said, "I don't smell anything."

We all were puzzled until Dawn realized we had brought the designed dummy sample of the bottle we planned to use and not the bottle with the perfume inside.

Needless to say, we all looked sheepish at first. Then we all burst out laughing, realizing we wanted to smell a fragrance, even if it wasn't there.

LESSON LEARNED

As everyone knows today: Never make a presentation to the executives who are in a position to decide your business future without first having a dry (perfume) run in order to be sure everything is in order.

Andy Warhol's Gift

I FIRST MET ANDY WARHOL while I was still at B. Altman & Co. It was January 15, 1975, the week before the announcement was made that I would be joining Bergdorf Goodman as the new president and CEO. The event was Halston's first menswear collection, presented at Lincoln Center's New York State Theater. I recall *Women's Wear Daily* describing the collection as extremely understated with major emphasis on jackets of Ultrasuede in a variety of colors.

What made this event remain in my mind was that every important retailer from New York City and throughout the United States was there, including the major merchandise executives from Bergdorf Goodman. No one in the audience, including the Bergdorf Goodman executives, knew the change that would take place in one of the most important fashion stores in the country. I knew that the following day's announcement of my new appointment was surely going to be one big surprise to all who were there that day. It was.

One of the high-profile attendees at the Halston show was Andy Warhol, who, everyone knew, was a friend of Halston and who brought additional attention to the show. I don't recall who introduced me to some of the guests at the show, but I do remember that one of those guests was Warhol. It

Andy Warhol. (Photo courtesy of Women's Wear Daily.*)*

was a brief introduction, and not necessarily memorable, except that once my appointment at Bergdorf Goodman was announced, and my business relations with Halston became active, Andy and I met on more than one occasion at different Halston events.

On one occasion, Bergdorf Goodman was planning a public relations event with Halston, which required Dawn Mello, Bergdorf's president; Susie Butterfield, the head of Bergdorf's PR; and me to meet with Warhol in his studio. After the meeting Warhol did a pencil sketch portrait of me and one of Dawn from a Polaroid shot that he took during the meeting. The Andy Warhol portrait hangs in my study to this day, reminding me of the excitement of bringing all the important fashion designers to Bergdorf Goodman and the personalities who joined in to raise the store to new heights.

LESSON LEARNED

Whenever an opportunity arises to meet an outstanding personality in business, art, or whatever field in which he or she might excel, always try to have a memento of the meeting, for future references and networking. At the very least, a business card will do.

Designer Frenzy

ROM THE MID-SEVENTIES into the mid-eighties, the Italians—Fendi, Armani, Albini, Basile, Cerruti, Ferragamo, Ferré, Missoni, and Versace—all became big fashion news and very successful financially. At the same time in Paris, Yves Saint Laurent with Rive Gauche, Karl Lagerfeld for Chanel, Claude Montana, Thierry Mugler, and Jean Paul Gaultier became great commercial success stories as well. Major fashion retailers recognized the tremendous acceptance of these fashion designers at prices, although expensive, that were far below the cost of their couture collections. They aggressively pursued every name fashion designer to be carried in their stores, striving for exclusive arrangements if possible and settling for semi-exclusive where necessary.

As noted in a *Women's Wear Daily* piece called "The Golden Gaffes of 1977," the frenzy created at Claude Montana's fashion show among others at "the tents" in Paris came close to riots as retailers with tickets, many friends of the designer, fashion press, and God only knows who else made it impossible to get into the shows.

At the Montana show, Marvin Traub, president of Bloomingdales; Ed Finkelstein, CEO of Macy's; Bob Suslow, CEO of Saks Fifth Avenue; Jerry Stutz, president of Henri

FROM LEFT TO RIGHT: *Gianni Versace, Valentino Garavani, Giorgio Armani, and Gianfranco Ferré. (Photo courtesy of* Women's Wear Daily.*)*

Bendel; and yours truly were all caught in the middle of the mob. It was all we could do to escape with our lives. Needless to say, we were unable to see the show.

Due to the newness, the frenzy was repeated at other shows as well, until professional guards were in place to help organize the unwieldy crowds. They were not much of an improvement.

The fashion designers, in many cases, thrived on the frenzy, creating excitement and public relations coverage for their collections. It would have been wise for all the major retailers collectively to have notified the fashion designers that they and their staffs would not attend until a more civilized approach was used to show their collections.

The caveat was that the designers then had the clue and the instinct to know that the retailers, press, notables. and friends

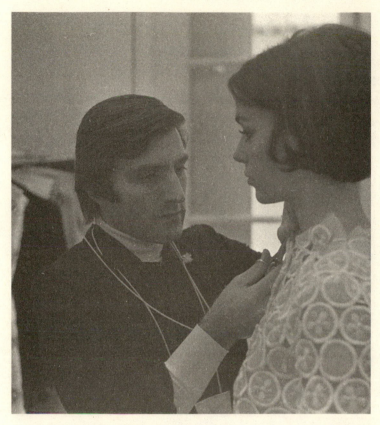

Emanuel Ungaro. (Photo © The New York Post.)

were afraid that they would miss something and miss being seen. And even today, a designer like Marc Jacobs can keep retailers and the fashion press cooling their heels for up to and sometimes more than an hour waiting for the collections to be shown.

As written in another chapter, "the fashion designers have taken charge." The large fashion shows were and are primarily for public relations. A great amount of press, many photographers, retail executives, and their entourage, in addition to the designer's friends, created mayhem.

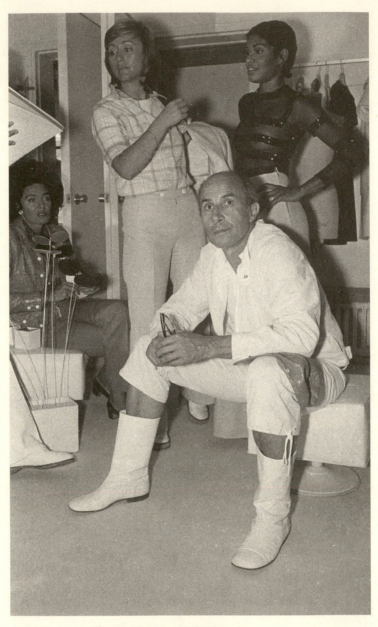

André Courrèges. (Photo © The New York Times.)

LESSON LEARNED
Since it is the fashion retailer's function to bring the newest and most exciting merchandise to its customers, experienced and professional buyers should, did, and do write their orders in the designer's showroom, quietly before or after all the hoopla at the fashion show for the press and for the crowd of whomsoever.

Hermès of Paris

THIS BOOK WOULD NOT BE COMPLETE without mentioning my experiences with Hermès, the great French luxury retailer. My first encounter with Hermès took place about 1973 when I was involved in upgrading B. Altman's grand main floor. With the removal of the food and notions departments, and a small U.S. Post Office to less important traffic areas in the store, there was room then for a luxury department such as Hermès. It would complement B. Altman's renowned main-floor gift department. My feeling was that Hermès would not be interested in a venture of this type and indeed my halfhearted effort never got very far.

About five years later, as the CEO of Bergdorf Goodman, when we reintroduced the French couture, Hermès President Jean-Louis Dumas approached me with his interest in Bergdorf Goodman's revival. His request for Hermès to have a shop on Bergdorf's main floor, facing Fifth Avenue, proved difficult.

At that time, Delman's leased shoe department occupied that prime real estate, with more than half of Bergdorf Goodman's Fifth Avenue frontage, including Delman's own entrance and display windows. Delman's had occupied this space for a very long time—possibly from the very beginning in 1927 when Edwin Goodman, Andrew's father, moved into the new building, replacing the Vanderbilt mansion.

This posed a unique problem. We had just completed an exclusive arrangement for the combination of Fendi handbags and furs. Fendi handbags were to have a dominant location in the remaining portion of Bergdorf's main floor that Delman's did not occupy. Fendi furs were to be carried in a special location in Bergdorf's fur department on the second floor. It was with great difficulty, as much as I admired Jean-Louis, and Hermès, not to be able to accommodate his proposal at that time.

A strange string of events with Hermès followed over the next few years. The first was the closing of Bonwit Teller's 57th Street store. Both Hermès and Turnbull & Asser, the luxury English men's retailer located there, were left with no retail space in New York City. With that situation, in my opinion untenable for Hermès (more about resolving the Turnbull & Asser situation in another chapter), I approached Jean-Louis with a proposal: Hermès could not be absent from New York City until it had a proper location. Until that time, Bergdorf Goodman would find an appropriate location to maintain elegant Hermès merchandise for his customers.

We found a reasonable location for Hermès tucked in Bergdorf's 58th Street rotunda entrance, and a 58th Street display window to match. There was even enough space to have a display counter of the famous "Claude," repairing Hermès merchandise for the entire world to see. In this arrangement of convenience, Bergdorf Goodman was also allowed to carry Hermès great silk ties in the men's department.

During this transition for Hermès, I tried any number of ways, unsuccessfully, to convince Jean-Louis that Bergdorf's would build a beautiful shop for Hermès, but not on Fifth Avenue. With Delman's and Fendi on Fifth, adding Hermès to whatever space was left would leave no representation for Bergdorf Goodman on Fifth Avenue. This did not make sense to me.

Within a few years after this arrangement of convenience, Hermès opened its own store on 57th Street. Bergdorf Goodman was able, however, to continue carrying Hermès ties in the men's department. Hermès business in its 57th Street store grew by leaps and bounds. A number of years later, it moved to its present location on Madison Avenue, now with a new Hermès men's store right across the street.

In 1992, after I had retired from Bergdorf Goodman, previous to Hermès moving from 57th Street, the president of Hermès of Paris (HOP, the American subsidy), Chris Fischer, resigned. On Christmas morning Jean-Louis called me from Paris: "Would you consider being the interim president of Hermès USA until Hermès selected a replacement for Mr. Fischer?" With great respect and admiration, I declined the position. I had only recently retired from Bergdorf Goodman. Over the past 50 years, getting up at 6:30 a.m. every morning and in many cases returning home 12 or more hours later was enough.

However, Jean-Louis did appoint me as a director of Hermès USA when I retired from Bergdorf Goodman. I volunteered to help oversee the transition of the new president, whomever it would be.

Shortly after, Laurent Mommeja, a young member of the Hermès family, was appointed to the presidency of HOP. My contribution at that time was to convince Jean-Louis of the need for Hermès to have a merchandise control procedure, similar to that used successfully in building Bergdorf Goodman's sales and profits. Jean-Louis agreed, and it was with the next appointment of Robert Chavez as the president of Hermès USA that the business really took off. Inventories have been managed remarkably well, as the sales and profits grew, also at a remarkable rate.

Welcome, Summer!

The season gets under way with celebrations
charitable, educational, theatrical, even personal.

ABOVE June 8, 7:20 P.M.: From left, BART OATES; TOMMY HILFIGER and his wife, SUSIE, and STEVE YOUNG were among nearly 800 guests at the Fresh Air Fund dinner saluting American heroes. More than $800,000 was pledged to benefit the fund, which has been providing free summer vacations for New York City children since 1877. The dinner-dance was held in a tent at Tavern on the Green in Central Park.

ABOVE June 2, 10 P.M.: From left, JANE GREENWOOD, the costume designer; ROBERT WHITEHEAD, the producer, and IRENE WORTH. Ms. Greenwood and her husband, Ben Edwards, the set designer, celebrated the marriage of their daughter Sara to Paul Manning at the Brooklyn Botanic Garden. RIGHT BEN EDWARDS with his niece MARY HARRIET SLINGLUFF.

LEFT June 6, 10:30 P.M.: After a performance of "Chronicle of a Death Foretold" to benefit Lincoln Center Theater, SANDRA GILMAN, left, greets LUIZ PEREZ, an actor, and GRACIELA DANIELE, director.

ABOVE June 7, 7:50 P.M.: From left, JACKIE NEIMARK; JEAN-LOUIS DUMAS-HERMES, chairman of the Colbert Foundation; KELLI QUESTROM and her husband, ALLEN, and COCO KOPELMAN at the foundation's dinner in the garden of the Cooper-Hewitt National Design Museum. The group promotes educational exchanges between France and the United States.

RIGHT 10 P.M.: TONYA PINKINS, left, a member of the cast, with IRA WEITZMAN, the music director, and LINDA LEROY JANKLOW, the chairwoman of the evening, which included an after-theater supper at the new Copacabana.

Photographs by BILL CUNNINGHAM/The New York Times

A fashionable week in early summer 1995, among nearly 800 guests who pledged more than $800,000 for the Fresh Air Fund at a Tavern on the Green dinner in Central Park.

CLOCKWISE FROM TOP LEFT: *Bart Oates, Tommy and Susie Hilfiger, and Steve Young; after a performance of* Chronicle of a Death Foretold *to benefit Lincoln Center for the Performing Arts,* Chronicle *costume designer Jane Greenwood, its producer Robert Whitehead, and Irene Worth; Ben Edwards with his niece Mary Harriet Slingluff; Sandra Gilman greeting* Chronicle *actor Luiz Perez and the show's director Graciela Daniele after their performance;* Chronicle *cast member Tonya Pinkins with music director Ira Weitzman and event chairwoman Linda Leroy Janklow; and at a Colbert Foundation dinner in the garden of the Cooper-Hewitt National Design Museum, Jackie Neimark, Jean-Louis Dumas (chairman of the Foundation), Kelli and Allen Questrom, and Coco Kopelman. (Photos by Bill Cunningham courtesy of* The New York Times.*)*

Jean-Louis Dumas opening the Hermès store in Beverly Hills.

The success of Hermès USA has been gratifying to me, as has been the success of Bergdorf Goodman. From the very beginning of my retail career, I observed people of wealth as customers, if treated with luxury, excellent service, and elegant merchandise, respond in the most favorable way. That is, they spend their money in good times and bad.

An excellent example of this in my mind was demonstrated during the recent recession. People have asked me, in sobering tones, "How was business at Hermès?" They were surprised with my positive response. During the worst time, business, even on Madison Avenue, was up, by single digits, compared to the major fashion retailers, who were experiencing sales declines of the magnitude not seen since the Great Depression.

The reason, I opined, was the difference of the ratio of the core customer at Hermès to other retailers. I believe the core customer at Hermès is about 90 percent and the "new achievers" would be about 10 percent. When the recession hit, the core customers may have bought a bit less, but it was the relatively small number of the "new achievers" at Hermès who dropped out of the market, who affected the smaller decline at Hermès.

It was the larger retailers, where I would hazard to guess the new achiever might have been as high as 50 percent, that caused major sales declines far greater than Hermès. This may have been proven during the fall of 2009, when Hermès was achieving substantial sales increases while major fashion retailer's sales continued to decline.

Hermès (HOP) today, under the direction of Robert Chavez as well as Hermès International, with Patrick Thomas as its chairman, continues to grow in all areas of this country and around the world. It is due to the elegant, luxury merchandise available to those customers who appreciate the best in quality workmanship and can afford it. This chapter would not be complete without a photograph including Hermès' Jean-Louis Dumas, who was also chairman of the Colbert Foundation. The foundation promotes educational exchange between France and the United States.

LESSONS LEARNED

My good fortune was to be associated with successful high-end luxury retailers, starting with my early introduction to Bonwit Teller, at a young and impressionable age, and continuing throughout my business career.

Wherever a person starts, aiming for excellence will always bring its rewards.

2

THE BUSINESS *of* FASHION

FASHION DESIGNER STORIES

The "Eye" for Fashion

THE LINCHPIN of Bergdorf Goodman's fashion strategy was our exceptional and creative fashion team. Heading up that team were Dawn Mello, fashion director and later president, and Barbara Lamonica, vice president and merchandise manager of Bergdorf's misses sportswear departments. Both had a very high batting average identifying the new exciting fashion designers.

They introduced me to Michael Kors, Donna Karan, Calvin Klein, and others who eventually became top headliners at Bergdorf Goodman. It was my job to convince the designers of the benefits of confining their collections exclusively to Bergdorf Goodman, or at least limiting their distribution among our competitors. Bergdorf Goodman's Fifth Avenue windows, dramatic fashion shows, and purchase orders as large as any of our competitors were a package difficult for them to turn down.

It was exciting as well as gratifying to see Bergdorf Goodman introduce Michael Kors's first collection in 1981. The collection was young and exciting—just like its designer. Michael was very enthusiastic about his introduction and first personal appearance. Needless to say, he and his collections were an instant success. His well-earned fashion reputation continued to grow, and he has become a dominant influence in the international world of fashion. I was always struck by Michael's clean American sportswear. He wanted his customers looking fine-tuned and just right. From his very beginning, he has been consistently consistent.

I followed Michael's career with great interest. Once again I had the opportunity to congratulate him personally when Jackie and I met him on a holiday. We were, by coincidence, staying at the same hotel in Capri, the Grand Hotel Quisisana. Even now, with his international fame, Michael, in accepting our praise, was as gracious as the first day I met him in Bergdorf Goodman.

An interesting sidelight: When two of my granddaughters living in Florida met Michael Kors at his fashion show in Palm Beach, he said to them, "I wouldn't be where I am today without your grandfather." Enough said.

LESSONS LEARNED

To be successful, a fashion business requires talented and creative people known for "having an eye."

The ability to discover a new and potentially future great fashion designer before your competition requires this very important gift.

Fashion Shows: Then and Now

AN INTERESTING CHANGE took place over the years with fashion designers' fashion shows. Relatively sedate showings evolved into extravaganzas. For example, Adele Simpson and Pauline Trigère presented their latest designs in relatively sedate occasions held right in the designers' showrooms, whereas today's top designers host events in giant tents or auditoriums of many sorts. The designer shows today invite hundreds of guests, including buyers, press, and friends. High-profile movie and television personalities are seated in the front rows to gain as much press exposure as possible. The music is so loud (to show that the designer is "with it") that no one can hear the person sitting next to him or her. Of course, you can't blame the designer; this is all done for the designer to get as much public relations exposure as possible. (Compare the striking difference of the two fashion shows illustrated on pages 126 and 127.)

Where designers in days gone by were concerned that someone might sketch a dress, today every garment shown is instantly shown around the world via computer, television, newspapers, and other types of media.

My Introduction to the Fashion
Designers of Days Gone By

GOING WAY BACK, when Roy Rudolph became the president of Bonwit Teller in 1948, I was appointed his assistant. This appointment was primarily due to my familiarity with the merchandising procedures of the store and the confidence the buyers had in me as the bridge between the Bill Holmes era and the new Walter Hoving ownership. Walter Hoving bought Bonwit Teller from Hortense Odlum's husband, Floyd Odlum, chairman of the Atlas Corporation. Unfortunately, Walter Hoving opened two large Bonwit Teller branches, one in Boston and the other (too quickly after the Boston opening) in Chicago; this expansion helped bring the luxury retail store to its demise.

Roy Rudolph knew of my interest not only in the figure end of the business but also in the fashion environment as well. Because of this interest, I was periodically invited to fashion shows held in the showrooms of the famous designers of the day, such as Adele Simpson, Pauline Trigère, Harvey Berin, Mollie Parnis, and Larry Aldrich.

In nearly every case, the designers' showrooms would seat approximately 50 people. The audience was made up of the important store presidents (CEO titles were still to come), their merchandise managers, and buyers. With soft background music, the style numbers were called out one by one by the designer or their assistants, as the models walked slowly down the short runway.

Adele was a rather small woman with the energy of a woman twice her size. The little gold chairs were set up the length of her beautifully decorated showroom, and Adele would fuss around her important customers and make everyone feel wanted and comfortable. The fashion show would last about a half hour, after which the presidents and their buyers, as was and still is the custom, would have the opportunity to congratulate the designers.

I single out Adele Simpson because she was my first introduction to the top fashion designers at that early time of my career. These shows, from Bonwit Teller through Bergdorf Goodman, left a lasting impression. They gave me

Chanel show, circa 2010. (Photo courtesy of Women's Wear Daily.*)*

Pauline Trigère show, circa 1970. (Photo courtesy of Women's Wear Daily.*)*

the taste level that allowed me to appreciate the later fashion designers who helped make Bergdorf Goodman the great store that it is today.

Pauline Trigère was the second fashion designer that I was fortunate to meet. Like Adele Simpson, she was one of the top fashion professionals of that time, but she added an exciting French temperament.

LESSON LEARNED

It can benefit your career early in the game if you can convince your superior (without a threat to his or her position) that it would be helpful for all concerned to meet the important players in your chosen field. Reason being to provide you with as complete an understanding as possible of the business and individuals at hand.

Caricature Snapshots of Designers I Have Known

Giorgio Armani

Low-key, high-profile, from bare bulb to the star in the spotlight.

Giorgio Armani fitting models for his Spring 1978 collection. (Photo by Tim Jenkins courtesy of Women's Wear Daily.*)*

Azzedine Alaia

First trip to Bergdorf Goodman wanted the Concorde, got first class, and is still first class.

Azzedine Alaia and Tina Turner at the 1986 French Gala in New York. (Photo by Eric Weiss courtesy of Women's Wear Daily.*)*

Geoffrey Beene

Always attempting for perfection and achieving it with graceful modernity.

Geoffrey Beene preparing for his ready-to-wear Spring/Summer 1972 show. (Photo by Nick Machalaba courtesy of Women's Wear Daily.*)*

Bill Blass

Society's designer, shrewd in business, willing to admit a mistake.

Bill Blass reads Women's Wear Daily *at home in 1962. (Photo by Troy Palmieri courtesy of* Women's Wear Daily.*)*

Pierre Cardin

Creatively commercial, led the way to licensing.

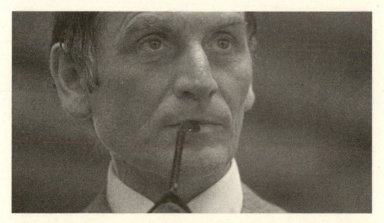

Pierre Cardin arriving from the Queen Elizabeth 2 *in New York, January 11, 1970. (Photo by Traina Sal courtesy of* Women's Wear Daily.*)*

Carolina Herrera

Elegant, elegant, elegant.

Carolina Herrera at the opening of the Metropolitan Museum of Art's exhibition on Yves Saint Laurent, December 12, 1983. (Photo by Tony Palmieri courtesy of Women's Wear Daily.*)*

Gianfranco Ferré

He wept when discovered. We wept when he died.

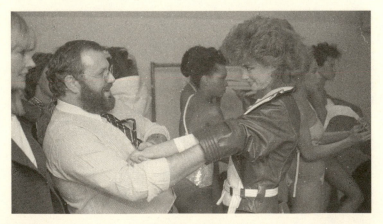

Gianfranco Ferré backstage with models at his Fall/Winter 1982 show. (Photo by Dustin Pittman courtesy of Women's Wear Daily.*)*

Isaac Mizrahi

First exclusive to Bergdorf Goodman, now to the world.

Isaac Mizrahi at the 2005 New York Botanical Garden's annual Orchid Dinner at the University Club. (Photo by Steve Eichner courtesy of Women's Wear Daily.*)*

James Galanos

Seemed to be above it all, but could read the bottom line.

James Galanos. (Photo by Jimi Celeste courtesy of Women's Wear Daily.*)*

Jean Paul Gaultier

Big man, big talent, big ideas.

Jean Paul Gaultier at the Fashion Group International's 20th Annual Night of Stars at Cipriani, New York City, October 30, 2003. (Photo by John Calabrese courtesy of Women's Wear Daily.*)*

Josie Natori

A class act for a top fashion designer and her ambition as a concert pianist.

Josie Natori. (Photo by Pasha Antonov courtesy of Women's Wear Daily.*)*

Hubert Givenchy

Great talent. Always gave the impression of surfacing from the court of Louis IV.

Hubert Givenchy in his studio showing pieces from his upcoming couture and ready-to-wear collections for Fall/Winter 1972. (Photo by Jean-Luce Huré courtesy of Women's Wear Daily.)

Halston

Brilliant, led down a different path by a conglomerate.

Roy Halston in his New York studio, June 15, 1973. (Photo by Traina Sal courtesy of Women's Wear Daily.)

Kasper

Low profile, always below the radar, but his name goes on forever.

Herbert Kasper attending a luncheon for designer Jackie Rogers thrown by Donald Brooks. (Photo by Harry Morrison courtesy of Women's Wear Daily.*)*

Fendi

The sisters, always looking for the best deal, usually found it.

Fendi sisters: Franco, Paola, Carla, Alda, and Anna (left to right) *with Karl Lagerfeld, 1983, Rome. (Photo © Corbis.)*

Marc Jacobs

Bloomed early and continues to grow.

Marc Jacobs, Spring 1987 RTW show. (Photo by George Chinsee courtesy of Women's Wear Daily.*)*

Mary McFadden

Adapted Grecian style, but always up-to-date.

Mary McFadden leaving the Carlyle at the Children's Home Benefit, October 29, 1975. (Photo by Sal Traina courtesy of Women's Wear Daily.*)*

Donna Karan

When she had a small business, small ego—now she has a large business.

Donna Karan at the opening of the Lord & Taylor store at White Flint shopping mall in Maryland, 1977. (Photo by Guy De Lort courtesy of Women's Wear Daily.*)*

Calvin Klein

Imaginative, creative, pushed his clothing rack all the way to the top.

Calvin Klein at home. (Photo by Thomas Iannaccone courtesy of Women's Wear Daily.*)*

Michael Kors

Central casting selection for talent and looks.

Michael Kors, Paris store. (Photo by Dominique Maitre courtesy Women's Wear Daily.*)*

Karl Lagerfeld

His words to me: "Better to be part of the change than to stand still." He never stood still.

Karl Lagerfeld, November 5, 1980. (Photo by Nick Machalaba courtesy of Women's Wear Daily.*)*

Ralph Lauren

Had the visions of a visionary, achieved the American dream for his customers and himself.

Ralph Lauren takes a bow at the end of his Fall/Winter collection runway show. (Photo by Troy Palmieri courtesy of Women's Wear Daily.*)*

Claude Montana

He really had it all and lost it all.

Claude Montana, Paris, October 1, 1996. (Gamma-Rapho via Getty Images.)

Oscar de la Renta
Learned design from the masters; became a master of design and business administration.

Oscar de la Renta in his New York office. (Photo by Nick Machalaba courtesy of Women's Wear Daily.*)*

Pauline Trigère
With a manager as strong as she was, would have been an even greater success.

Adele Simpson, Larry Aldrich, and Pauline Trigère watching the Bergdorf Goodman Plaza Collection show for Resort, 1973. (Photo by Peter Simins courtesy of Women's Wear Daily.*)*

Jerry Silverman and Shannon Rogers

Very talented, very successful, and very generous.

New York City Mayor John Lindsay, Councilwoman Carol Greitzer, Jerry Silverman, and Abe Schrader in 1972, changing Seventh Avenue to "Fashion Avenue" in the Garment District of Manhattan. (Photo courtesy of Women's Wear Daily.*)*

Ungaro

Personable as he was talented. We never really said good-bye.

Emanuel Ungaro at his Spring/Summer ready-to-wear show in New York, 1968. (Photo by Sal Traina courtesy of Women's Wear Daily.*)*

Valentino

Brought Italian couture to Paris with imperial success.

Valentino Garavani in his studio. (Photo by Moe Becker courtesy of Women's Wear Daily.*)*

Yves Saint Laurent

The quiet genius who communicated through his creativity.

Yves Saint Laurent at a party, 1972. (Photo by Pierre Schermann courtesy of Women's Wear Daily.)

Donna Karan

I HAVE WRITTEN ABOUT OBSERVING American fashion designers grow over the years. Geoffrey Beene grew when he started his career as draper for the American fashion designer Teal Traina, as did Oscar de la Renta for Ben Shaw, as did Donald Brooks and Halston. Even Ralph Lauren began his great career by selling his own designer neckties.

There are many more fashion designers, of course, all achieving international fame and business success. But being present at the birth of Donna Karan's fashion designer business demonstrates what a fashion concept, professional management, and proper financing can achieve.

The Donna Karan story is an example of how a great designing talent within a relatively short time gained fame, fortune, and international status as well. I first met Donna Karan when she was part of the design team at Anne Klein. She and Louis Dell'Olio showed great talent. The Anne Klein collections were a fine business for those stores that had a growing upscale business.

It became apparent to Dawn Mello and me during the late seventies and early eighties when we were building and acquiring fashion designer collections for Bergdorf Goodman that Donna Karan, under her own label, could be a star. At various times,

Dawn and I at first hinted and then Dawn strongly influenced Donna to have her own design house. We would commit to her business with strong purchases, high-profile fashion shows, Fifth Avenue window displays, and a dominant Donna Karan shop in a prime location. Our commitment to Donna, of course, meant that Donna in turn would commit to us: her personal appearance trunk (fashion) show each season would appear exclusively at Bergdorf Goodman in New York City.

We went a bit further by my contacting the CEO of Neiman Marcus at that time, recommending to him, with the combined buying power of Neiman Marcus and Bergdorf Goodman, that we could negotiate an exclusive arrangement to launch Donna Karan in the United States. I prefer not to mention the CEO's name, as he turned the idea down and, in the vernacular of that time, I felt that he blew it.

Nevertheless, one day Donna and her husband, Stephan Weiss, a wonderful fellow with no retail or wholesale background but a very savvy and talented businessman, came to visit me regarding their plan to start their own business.

I advised them that they would be a great success—with one caveat. With Donna's design talent a foregone conclusion, she must make timely delivery of her merchandise to her retail accounts. This was imperative for her success.

Fast delivery to the selling floor of Bergdorf's, Bloomingdales, and Saks of key lines like Donna's, Armani, and Calvin Klein became so competitive; at stake was which store could present these lines first. The management of the stores allowed the merchandise to bypass their marking rooms. The price tickets went on the items right on the selling floor.

Both Donna and Stephan acknowledged the fact, but unfortunately, with all Donna's success, her deliveries never quite equaled her other outstanding qualities.

Donna started her own design house with, in my opinion, two of the smartest men in the business: Tomio Taki and Frank Mori. Both were well-financed, experienced professionals. Their combination with Donna's and Stephan's talents brought about instant success, fame, and fortune.

LESSONS LEARNED

Being able to recognize talent, designers and otherwise, is a gift. If used wisely, it can bring great rewards to all concerned.

To be recognized requires the ability to demonstrate your talent in any manner that will make the powers that be aware of your future potential.

THE ENTREPRENEURS

Pioneers of American Apparel

A S A MERCHANDISING CLERK at Bonwit Teller before WWII, I was fortunate to be invited by the handbag buyer Regina Hellman to go into the handbag market with her. I was intrigued even then to see three of the most prominent luxury handbag manufacturers of those days— Koret, Pichel, and Coblentz. They were relatively small but creative manufacturers and designers that dominated the handbag market. Those names, known in the luxury market to relatively few people, mainly their upscale customers, were proudly embossed inside their handbags. There were others, of course, such as Morris White, that were more popularly priced and widely distributed.

I say I was intrigued because I had watched over the years as handbags, an important fashion accessory, were the domain of a relatively small group of manufacturers and witnessed how they became explosive in their growth with the rise of the fashion designers. Handbags as a fashion accessory took on a completely new dynamic, with every fashion designer featuring his or her "designer bag."

It was also during this time that small, individual women's apparel entrepreneurs started to manufacture dresses, coats, suits, and blouses. In the beginning they sold to department and specialty stores, and during the war manufactured, in many cases, uniforms for the armed forces. They too, as will be shown, experienced the same transformation and evolution, from small entrepreneurs to designer houses and then on to conglomerates. They reached to heights never imagined by the founders of these small businesses.

World War II cut off the fashion creativity from Europe, particularly Paris, requiring and giving the opportunity to American designers to come into their own. It was after the war and into the early fifties that these and other manufacturers began to dominate their moderate price markets. A few examples:

- Dresses—R&K, Leslie Fay, Jonathan Logan, Abe Schrader, and Puritan Fashions
- Blouses—Judy Bond
- Suits—S. Augustine (Palm Beach Suits)

Then the so-called better dress and sportswear markets were developed by designer houses such as Claire McCardell, Anne Fogarty, Bonnie Cashin, Adele Simpson, Harvey Berin, Larry Aldrich, Mollie Parnis, Jerry Silverman, and B. H. Wragge, to name an important few. At various times, all were carried in Bergdorf Goodman.

In those days, department and specialty stores usually had their apparel departments segregated first by floor, then by misses or women's departments on each floor. In some cases, stores were arranged in reverse, with the moderate-priced apparel departments on the lower floors, higher prices on the middle floors, and budget departments on the upper floors.

There were also department stores that had "Bargain Basements." These were eventually handed over "as a gift" to the newly emerging discount stores. One of the exceptions to this decision was the brilliance of Filene's Basement. These merchants recognized that well-to-do customers always liked a bargain and lower-priced customers always needed a bargain.

On each of the moderate, better, and budget floors, misses and women's dress, coats, and suit departments were all separated from each other. The junior departments were conveniently (usually by design) located somewhere else.

Sweaters, blouses, and skirts were in their own departments. Sportswear, as we know it today, was yet to come. And designer sportswear was yet to come after that.

Today that has all changed. No longer in major department stores and large specialty stores are there dress, coat, suit, and blouse or sweater departments with anywhere from 10 to 20 different manufacturers making up the department's assortment. Now in these stores, designer shops with dresses, coats, suits, sportswear, and whatever are all under the designer's name in its own shops.

These early apparel manufacturers were all colorful characters. Perhaps they had to be to survive and grow very successfully in the highly competitive, and at times helter-skelter, marketplace.

LESSON LEARNED

I always greatly admired the men and women who built the apparel business in America to what it is today. Many arrived in this country with nothing and built apparel empires that serve as business models today.

The Dauphins of Seventh Avenue

I WRITE FIRST ABOUT MY EXPERIENCES with the fathers of these companies who taught me the rules of the game and then their successful sons, whom I have dubbed the "dauphins of Seventh Avenue." The Seventh Avenue dauphins that I have written about have left the industries of their fathers (and grandfathers) to become great successes on their own.

Fred Pomerantz and John Pomerantz

When I arrived at Gladdings, in Providence, Rhode Island, in 1951 after "growing up" at Bonwit Teller, I was not familiar with the lower-priced dress markets. The first manufacturer who taught me the ropes of this priced market was Fred Pomerantz of Leslie Fay Co. Whenever I visited his company, I knew he was there when I saw his Rolls-Royce parked in front of 500 Seventh Avenue, where he would invite me to lunch from time to time at the 500 Club.

His son, John, joined the Leslie Fay Company in 1960 right after he graduated from the Wharton School at University of Pennsylvania. John and I have known each other from his early days, and we reminisce from time to time about how his father and their old New England salesman, Mr. Fudderman, bailed me out of my merchandising mistakes. John became president in 1972 and continued to build the business, first by having the right merchandise at the right time and then, nearly equally as important, by developing close personal relationships with CEOs and buyers of all the stores with whom he did business.

In the eighties there was a leveraged buyout of the company, and many other financial and management changes took place during the eighties and nineties. In fact, there were so many that I lost track of the company and its many divisions, but I always retained a friendly relationship with John from our early years.

David Schwartz and Richard Schwartz

I became familiar with the Jonathan Logan Company and its owner, David Schwartz, also in the fifties. I was then the merchandise manager of women's apparel for Gladdings in Providence and later G. Fox & Co. in Hartford. It was my habit to accompany the buyers of my divisions whenever they were making the buy from our important manufacturers. (Please note, I didn't write "designer" houses in this case.) David Schwartz was a no-nonsense apparel manufacturer who, when I came to his showroom, literally pushed the salesman aside and took over. And a great and aggressive salesman he was.

Richard, his son, was made head of Jonathan Logan in the late sixties. By 1966 Jonathan Logan had become one of the largest ready-to-wear companies in the United States. They owned companies such as Youth Guild and Butte Knit.

An interesting aside: Liz Claiborne began a 15-year career as chief designer for Youth Guild, where she spent years unsuccessfully trying to convince top executives that there was a need for mix-and-match coordinated sportswear that would appeal to the growing numbers of women like herself who were not content to stay at home. When she left Youth Guild,

Ms. Claiborne started her own business in 1976 with $50,000 in personal savings and $200,000 from family and friends. It was an immediate hit, and within a decade, Liz Claiborne made it into *Fortune* magazine's list of the 500 largest companies in the United States. In 1985, the Schwartz family sold their interest in the Jonathan Logan Company.

Here too I have maintained a long-time, cordial relationship with Dick Schwartz. He and his wife, Sheila, were nice enough to have a dinner party for Jackie and me to introduce us to members of Century Golf Club when we applied for membership.

Abe Schrader and Mort Schrader

Abe Schrader was the last of the greats. He began in the garment business as a contract jobber, and in 1952, he formed the Abe Schrader Corporation. His Seventh Avenue ready-to-wear house made upscale dresses, coats, and suits for women. His head designer was Belle Saunders. I should add here that at the time Abe Schrader's dresses would have been carried in the store's dress department, coats in the coat departments, and suits in the suit departments.

If today, as explained above, Abe Schrader's designer was to have a Belle Saunders shop, then dresses, coats, and suits would all be together in her shop. By the seventies, this "designer shop" concept was the beginning of the seismic shift in the retail apparel business.

Mort, Abe's son, entered the business also in the sixties. With his father, Mort Schrader built one of the most successful apparel businesses on Seventh Avenue. By a lucky coincidence for me, Mort married Miquette Viterbo, the daughter of the family who owned Tiktiner, the French apparel company in Nice. Tiktiner was one of Bergdorf Goodman's major European designers. Mort, Miquette, and I through this relationship were able to maintain a friendship over the years.

Abe Schrader sold his business to Interco in 1984. Mort Schrader went on to be a very successful real-estate executive with PBS Realty Advisors.

Laurence (Larry) Leeds

Manhattan Industries was founded in 1857 by the grandfather of Laurence Leeds. I first met Larry and his cousin, Robert, when I was the general merchandise manager of B. Altman & Co. Larry had taken sole control of the company in the mid-seventies after Robert left. The company initially famously concentrated on men's dress shirts. Under Larry Leeds's management, the company branched out into other types of businesses, including Frost Brothers Stores, the Henry Grethel collections, and Perry Ellis.

Larry left Manhattan Industries in the early nineties following a hostile takeover of the company. He then entered the investment industry. He now is the chairman of Buckingham Capital.

Ben Shaw and Gerald Shaw

Ben Shaw was a legendary garment district entrepreneur and power broker. He gained his reputation by helping to launch the careers for designers such as Donald Brooks, Norman Norell, Stephen Burrows, Giorgio di Sant'Angelo, and Halston.

In 1965 Ben and his son Gerald recruited Oscar de la Renta from Elizabeth Arden. The company was later restructured as Oscar de la Renta Ltd. and fashion history was made.

Jerry Shaw retired as president and vice chairman in 1964. Oscar appointed the company's general counsel, Jeffry Aronsson, to be the company's new CEO. Jeffry Aronsson's tenure was marked, in addition to other successes, by multiplying the size of the company's business through an overhaul of its operations, and by building a reputation for improving the image of its product through disciplined licensing arrangements that have helped make the Oscar de la Renta the fashion designer and brand name. It is, in my opinion, possibly one of the last of the great luxury fashion designers on Seventh Avenue.

The Dauphine of Seventh Avenue

I would be remiss without mentioning a dauphine, Joan Raines, the daughter of Adele Simpson. Adele Simpson was called "the little lady with big ideas." One of the first American women to become a leading fashion designer started in the apparel business as a Seventh Avenue designer in 1921 when she was 17. Her dresses were sold in the finest stores in America. She remained active in the business for almost 60 years, running her own company, Adele Simpson Inc. Her daughter, Joan Raines, one of the few female executives of those years, joined the company in 1963 and ran it successfully until she sold it in 1980 to Baron Peters, another apparel company, no longer in business.

LESSONS LEARNED

"The apple doesn't fall far from the tree" is a proper adage for the dauphins. The family environment and business surroundings helped to shape their future careers. However, those of us who were fortunate to know their fathers, mothers, and the dauphins themselves were also exposed to the opportunities available to us.

Those who took advantage of the opportunities prospered. Those who did not were relegated to mediocrity.

It also helps to have a rich father.

Fashion Designers as Brands

THE POSITION that Bergdorf Goodman took in 1983 to discontinue carrying Halston's ready-to-wear and cosmetics was a reaction to the designer's licensing his name to JCPenney, where he was to design moderate apparel and other merchandise. Halston's decision was met in the fashion world with dismay. Even today I am often asked why such drastic action was taken, when today it is considered the normal route for a designer to take to expand his or her business as brands.

Starting in 1975, Bergdorf Goodman's merchandising strategy was to aggressively promote those fashion designer collections that were neglected previous to my arrival. That strategy was based on selling exclusive and semi-exclusive designer collections that were to be carried by Bergdorf Goodman. Either Bergdorf Goodman carried them alone—such as the combination of Fendi furs and leather goods, Halston, Geoffrey Beene, Issey Miyaki, Krizia, and too many more to be listed here—or semi-exclusively—such as Armani, Rive Gauche by Yves Saint Laurent, and many others that were carried by Bloomingdales, some at Saks, and possibly at Bendel and Barneys.

Carrying these designer collections in broad assortments and in depth, as well as being heavily promoted with newspaper and magazine advertising, Fifth Avenue windows, and fashion shows, brought Bergdorf Goodman closer to being number one on Fifth Avenue. In addition, the fashion designers benefited greatly. They had tremendous exposure through Bergdorf's efforts, allowing them to look around and discover that, in many cases, their names were more important to their customers from a high-fashion point of view than many of the retailers who just carried their collections.

The fashion designers' next step was to open their own shops, while the larger fashion retailers kept promoting them, making their merchandise more desirable than ever. With this exclusive/semi-exclusive strategy in place, working so successfully for Bergdorf Goodman with the fashion designers in the eighties, further distribution in the New York area would negate, to some degree, our successful growth.

Halston's surprising celebration party held at the Museum of Natural History announcing his arrangement with JCPenney did not fit into Bergdorf Goodman's exclusive/semi-exclusive marketing strategy. We felt, with the time, money, promotion, and real estate devoted to help Halston become a celebrity and to build his fashion reputation, Halston selling merchandise with the Halston label to a lower-priced volume retailer would allow that popular-priced retailer to benefit from Bergdorf Goodman's fashion reputation, and the many years of expensive promotional efforts. Having a Halston boutique at Bergdorf Goodman as well as having Halston merchandise at JCPenney didn't make smart merchandising sense to me.

That was then. Now is now.

Since that time, fashion designers, first, with tremendous success, opened their own shops on every important avenue and shopping center around the world. Second, they began licensing their names to what was then called secondary lines.

With continued success, they also opened closeout stores (with merchandise in most cases made only for those stores).

The final innovation for the designers was to follow the Halston business model, 20 years later. Today any number of fashion designers, many successfully, are designing collections for large volume discount stores.

With fashion designers' names being exposed at so many different levels, they are considered brand names. The question remains, will this overexposure of fashion designers as brand names at some point turn the luxury fashion customer off?

LESSON LEARNED
Is there ever too much of a good thing?

The Lauders

E VERY CAREER, TO BE SUCCESSFUL, is influenced not only by circumstances but also by people who are inspirational. There were a good number of individuals who inspired me to work to the best of my ability, but throughout my business career, to my good fortune, there was one family in particular. The Lauders.

I first met Estée and Joseph Lauder in the early sixties when I became the general merchandise manager of G. Fox & Co. in Hartford, Connecticut. Late one afternoon Jackie and I drove down from Hartford to the Plaza Hotel in New York, where we were invited to a gala party hosted by Estée and Joe. We were not exactly country bumpkins but were awed by the other guests, from the top retailers in the country, fashion magazine editors, business executives, and, of course, the fashion press. Estée always knew how to throw a party. What stayed in my mind all these years were the elegant and expensive gifts given to all the guests—not looked upon today as good form but great public relations then.

It was my opinion (possibly influenced by the enthusiasm of the guests, all of whom could have easily afforded to buy the gifts) that Estée developed her market-shaking idea, "Gift With Purchase." This revolutionary marketing concept swept through not only the cosmetic industry but other industries as well. I have often thought the airlines adopted the practice of mileage points from Estée Lauder's big idea as well.

I mentioned being influenced by circumstances and people. Early on I could see that I could learn a lot from Estée Lauder: how she marketed her products and her strong competitive nature, particularly with her intense rivalry with Charles Revson, and, I might add, anyone else who was unfortunate enough to get in her way.

One of Estée's early ideas that made a lasting impression on me went something like this: "Put on a new face for the New Year." January, she explained, was one of the quietest months to sell cosmetics and she wanted her customers to have a reason to spend their money with her after Christmas as well as before.

It worked.

From then on, I was always asking my people for promotional ideas that would make our customer think of Bergdorf Goodman every day of their busy lives.

I often tell the story of Estée and all the Lauder clan descending on me at B. Altman & Co. and she demanding what was considered to be the prime location in the newly built cosmetic department. Estée, as usual, got her prized front and center location. Her saying of "Location, location, location" is as valid today as it was then.

A few years later when I was the CEO at Bergdorf Goodman, Estée Lauder visited her department frequently

FROM LEFT TO RIGHT: *Ira Neimark and William and Estée Lauder at Bergdorf Goodman. (Photo by Robert Mitra courtesy of* Women's Wear Daily.*)*

for two reasons. The first, I am pleased to say, was to shop for herself throughout the store. The second, she explained to me, was to visit and build her own line's presence in the store. Her office and headquarters were located across Fifth Avenue in the General Motors building. Estée wanted to be sure that when retailers came to New York, they would see at Bergdorf Goodman an example of what she was proud of (a tough accomplishment). Therefore, it was my responsibility to see to it that Bergdorf Goodman represented all the Estée Lauder lines in the best manner possible. In the process, inch-by-inch and eventually foot-by-foot, Estée Lauder and her other cosmetic lines gained enough counter space to have the largest cosmetic department in the store. And, I might add, all other stores as well.

Fast-forward to 1990. Due to Estée and her enormously talented son, Leonard, the Estée Lauder Company had grown and prospered to be one of the largest cosmetic companies in the world. The company aggressively expanded into major retailers not considered in the early growing years, and added new lines such as Origins, with many more to come. I mention Origins to show how the passing of the torch from one generation to another can be successfully accomplished when planned early on, instead of in haste.

The Origins marketing concept was similar to the launching strategy of Guerlain a number of years before at Bergdorf Goodman and Bobbi Brown in 1990 as well. Their marketing strategy? Launch the newly introduced brand exclusively at Bergdorf Goodman, the highest-profile and most prestigious store. After the successful initial impact, other retailers and their customers will be clamoring for the merchandise.

Obviously, it worked to everyone's satisfaction. Well, I am sorry to say, everyone except one. By now, my very good and long-standing friend Estée Lauder attended the launch of Origins, marketed by her grandson, William; she was concerned that the Origins counters were better positioned and possibly overshadowed her very own Estée Lauder counters, her favorite from her very beginning. Needless to say, she let her displeasure be known. Estée Lauder never, ever gave up.

The lady taught me a lot. Be competitive, be creative, and be inspirational to your people.

LESSONS LEARNED

In every company, large and small, there are business relationships with other companies that will be led by outstanding executives with inspirational qualities.

It is important to identify these people. Slowly but surely, let them become aware of your interest in their accomplishments and your own ambitions.

DEALS AND DIPLOMACY

The Gimbel Saks Buying Office and Bergdorf Goodman

W HEN I JOINED Bergdorf Goodman in 1975, I was confronted with a competitive alliance. This concerned me regarding the independence of Bergdorf's buying organization in the European fashion markets.

Gimbels and Saks, many years earlier due to their family relationships, formed the Gimbel Saks buying office. Their foreign headquarters and large buying staff were located in Paris. The office was very successful, with the buying power and association with large stores such as Gimbel Brothers and the prestigious Saks Fifth Avenue. The Broadway Stores, now Carter Hawley Hale, were located mainly in California. They were not in the major competitive areas with Gimbels or Saks but were also a member of the buying office.

The Broadway Stores bought (and merged with) Neiman Marcus in the late sixties and Bergdorf Goodman in the early seventies. Both stores were required to use the Gimbel Saks buying office for their European purchases. This posed a great dilemma for me, with my business strategy, for the want of better words, to take on my main competitors, Saks Fifth Avenue, Bloomingdales, and Henri Bendel.

In my opinion, having Saks with its large buying power in the same buying office as Bergdorf Goodman put Bergdorf's ability to attract French and Italian designer collections to a distinct disadvantage.

This was proven to me very obviously on two occasions. The first I would attribute to my lack of European buying experience as well as being a bit naïve. In my initial request to bring Yves Saint Laurent's Rive Gauche to Bergdorf Goodman, I requested Jean Bujon, the president of the Gimbel Saks office, to arrange an interview for us to meet with Pierre Bergé, the principal of YSL. The objective was to convince Mr. Bergé to sell the Rive Gauche collection to Bergdorf Goodman.

Mr. Bujon, of course, was very concerned with Bergdorf Goodman going after one of Saks Fifth Avenue's major accounts. Thus, he made the introduction to Mr. Bergé one of the shortest business meetings of my career. It dawned on me that Bergdorf Goodman was considered a second-class citizen in the Gimbel Saks office.

The second experience was the reverse. With much effort and persuasion, I was able to bring Charvet, the great French men's haberdasher, to Bergdorf Goodman. We had been granted an exclusive arrangement with our commitment to Denis Colban for a Charvet shop in the men's department, similar to his store in Paris.

One morning as I was leaving the Ritz Hotel, I saw Jean Bujon with Burt Tansky, then the president of Saks Fifth Avenue, passing the hotel (without them seeing me), on their way to Charvet, across the Place Vendôme. *Here we go again*, I thought. Jean Bujon was escorting Burt Tansky, one of my main competitors, to meet Denis Colban, the owner of

Charvet, one of Bergdorf Goodman's exclusive collections. Mr. Colban asked me later whether I would have a problem if, through the introduction by the Gimbel Saks office, Saks was to carry his collections. My answer, of course, was yes, I did have a problem. I didn't need my buying office to take my competitor from the same office to a men's fashion house where Bergdorf Goodman had an exclusive arrangement. Saks did not get the line until a few years later. It wasn't successful at Saks, as I'd told Mr. Colban that it wouldn't be, and was dropped.

Years later, as exclusive arrangements became harder to maintain, Charvet was carried in Bergdorf Goodman, also Neiman Marcus, and finally again at Saks Fifth Avenue. Bob Suslow, who had become the chairman of Saks, asked why I was so dissatisfied with his buying office. I explained that I was paying the same percentage fee as Saks, but Bergdorf's was not getting 100 cents on the dollar of service as they were.

Fortunately, when Bergdorf Goodman's ownership went to General Cinema in 1987, I requested and was granted the right for Bergdorf Goodman to leave the Gimbel Saks office. My recommendation was for Caryl Actis-Grande and her husband, Dick, to start their own office exclusively for Bergdorf Goodman, Neiman Marcus, and Holt Renfrew. This decision proved to be a great and enduring success for all concerned.

This was also very fortunate timing. The Gimbel Saks office went into some type of reorganization about that time. That would have left Bergdorf Goodman and Neiman Marcus high and dry without a buying office. Once again the pinball bounced in the right direction.

LESSON LEARNED

When you are developing a business plan, it is critical to know all the players and how each, in turn, will fit into making your strategy and business model a success. Like chess or checkers, be aware of each player's goals and be sure their moves benefit your objectives, not theirs.

Meeting Financial Leaders

WHILE BUILDING BERGDORF GOODMAN, in addition to meeting the many fashion designers and the high-profile social celebrities, there were occasions that brought me into contact with the financial movers and shakers of that time and into the present.

Henry Kravis and Carolyne Roehm

When Henry Kravis was married to Carolyne Roehm, they had to decide whom to appoint as the head of Carolyne's fashion design house. Henry called me at Bergdorf's and asked if he and Carolyne could meet with me for my opinion. They related the problems they were having, mainly inventory-related. They found a manager that they were interested in and wanted to know if I had any experience with the executive in my normal course of business.

When they mentioned the candidate's name, they could see my instant surprise. This was the same executive who when Yves Saint Laurent's perfume, Opium, was launched in New York made the decision that Bloomingdales and Bendel should have the launch, excluding Bergdorf Goodman. This was a marketing decision that even Pierre Bergé, the head

SanfordWeill in his new office and fireplace on the 106th floor at 2 World Trade Center, March 2, 1981. (Photo courtesy of New York Daily News *via Getty Images.)*

of Yves Saint Laurent, recognized as needing rectification—particularly since Bergdorf's had just introduced Yves Saint Laurent's couture collection. He did so by sending packages of Opium perfume directly from Paris to Bergdorf Goodman.

I found that when people ask for recommendations or references, the less said, the better. However, it is quite proper to relate your experience with the executive in question and let the inquirer make his or her own decision. In this particular case, I understood that the candidate was hired and it turned out to be less than a successful appointment.

Sandy Weill

Sandy Weill and I first met when he had a brief exposure to the luxury designer business. He was the chairman of

American Express in 1983 and in 1984 chairman of the executive committee.

An article in *Women's Wear Daily*, March 29, 1984, reads: "American Express's unlikely staging of a New York City Breakers performance in the gilded halls of the Cercle d' Interallie, one of Paris' stuffiest clubs." Sandy also hosted a dinner party for fashion executives in Paris for the prêt-à-porter collections, at the magnificent apartment of Edmund and Lily Safra.

Stephen Schwarzman

In 1991, Stephen Schwarzman, cofounder, president, and CEO of the Blackstone Group, posed with me in a photograph for a piece on men's fashions in *The New York Times* that announced the opening of Bergdorf Goodman's Men's Store. Mr. Schwarzman was one of the many financial celebrities who helped to launch Bergdorf Goodman's Men's Store as the premier shopping experience for many famous executives.

LESSONS LEARNED

Although mentioned previously, this lesson is so important that it bears repeating. In recruiting top management executives, it is imperative to research all the people (reliable) and all the performance records available, in order to be sure the final decision will benefit you and your business. It is better to make no move at all than to make the mistake of selecting the wrong person.

Whenever possible, in order to promote your business, it helps to have highly recognizable celebrities, financial or otherwise, involved. Needless to say, the business has to be recognized as worthy as its association.

Ira Neimark and Stephen A. Schwarzman featured in The New York Times'
Men's Fashion of the Times.

Ribbon cutting, Bergdorf Goodman's Men's Store. (Photo courtesy of Ira Neimark.)

Ira Neimark inspecting the final touches of the new Bergdorf Goodman's Men's Store. (Photo by Burke Uzzle courtesy of The New York Times.*)*

Harrods and Mohamed Al-Fayed

OVER THE YEARS as I made my semiannual trips to Europe, even though Bergdorf Goodman's heaviest buying was done in Milan and Paris, I would always travel to London to visit with Delman Shoes, Turnbull & Asser, and Penhaligon's. These three companies didn't require my presence, but I found them to be always interesting, enjoyable, and all typically British.

Delman was headed up by Edward Rayne, a very colorful English gentleman who was knighted in 1990. Delman held the ladies' shoe department lease at Bergdorf Goodman. I was very unhappy about it and worked toward its being discontinued at the earliest possible time. I always enjoyed Eddie's company, and even though we never agreed that Delman was a fashionable shoe department, we still got along. Eddie was appointed to head up the British Fashion Guild and was instrumental in Jackie and my being invited to the evenings with Princess Diana and Prime Minister Thatcher.

Ken Williams headed up Turnbull & Asser and is a very colorful character. He truly epitomized what England was and is all about. In addition to operating one of the best and most famous men's shops in the world, Ken was socially connected through the royal family. It was through Ken and his association with Princess Diana that my golf game was arranged at Windsor Castle. Whenever I toured Turnbull for ideas, I recall hearing Ken greeting titled royal customers "Good afternoon, Your Grace." A real British environment, most impressive.

With the closing of Bonwit Teller, Turnbull & Asser also lost its location in New York. Our negotiating with Ken convinced him that Bergdorf Goodman, not Bloomingdales or Saks, would make the proper home for T&A. Many years later as exclusivity changed, T&A now sells to those stores as well.

Turnbull & Asser was bought in the eighties by Ali Al-Fayed, brother of Mohamed. Mohamed then owned Harrods in London and the Hotel Ritz in Paris, two of my most enjoyable destinations in Europe. The Al-Fayed ownership of Turnbull and their appreciation of the talents of Ken Williams led to my being introduced to both Al-Fayed brothers and to my introduction to Harrods. Whenever I traveled to London, I always visited the famed emporium, as did every retailer from around the world.

There was great contention in England when Al-Fayed bought Harrods, but I won't go into that. Nevertheless, Mohamed bought the giant of a store that required a lot of work for it to be more than a big store. It had a great assortment of merchandise, from christening clothes to funeral arrangements and everything in between.

I had met Mohamed at different business and social functions in and out of Harrods, and was invited to meet with him in his office around 1987. He asked me to tour the store and give him my impressions. I did (not too favorable given the then-current trend in retailing.) Somewhere along the line he asked if I would consider working for him. I thanked him and responded that I was very pleased with my present arrangement with Bergdorf Goodman. However, I would be available to him to answer any questions that he might have regarding retailing in general.

During our meeting in his office, his secretary came in and said that the president of Jenny, at that time a very important Italian fashion design company, had come in and wished to say hello. Mohamed said to send him in. When he entered the office, Mohamed said, "We do a big job with this company, I am sure much larger than Bergdorf Goodman." The president of Jenny said, "No, Bergdorf Goodman does a much bigger job than Harrods." I thought Mohamed would go ballistic. He shouted to his secretary to get the buyer and the merchandise manager into his office and proceeded to raise the roof. "Why would a small store on Fifth Avenue do more business than Harrods?" I don't recall their answer, but I felt it was time for me to leave.

Mohamed Al-Fayed always struck me as a businessman who was determined to be number one. He has taken Harrods to being not only one of the largest stores in the world but one of the most successful retail entities in the world as well.

Mohamed's many courtesies included sending his car for Jackie and me when we were in Paris at that time to have a private tour of the home of the late Duke and Duchess of Windsor, which he owned. A most memorable visit.

LESSON LEARNED

Always take the opportunity to visit every business that relates to your own. The networking of meeting one executive and then being introduced to the next is like compound interest. Your business relationships will grow and grow.

3

THE FALL *of* SERVICE

THE LOST ART OF CUSTOMER SERVICE

When Opportunity Knocks

A T THE BEGINNING OF THIS BOOK I wrote about leaving high school to go to work to help my family during the Great Depression. One of the major benefits for me was to be exposed to successful executives and to observe how they operated. This education began at the age of 17. I exchanged one type of classroom for another and never looked back.

Early on, I noticed that ambitious executives made great efforts to establish important business contacts and business relationships, building what today are called networks, or connections, via the process of networking. For one executive to call another regarding a request for one reason or another, possibly for an introduction to someone in his network, is regarded in my book as a business opportunity. I mention these business/social relationships because I saw this practice bring about many successful careers. Needless to say, I too adopted the business relationships with anyone I thought could help advance my young career. This, by my definition, is opportunism.

A good example happened early in my career, when I moved from Bonwit Teller in New York to join Gladdings, in Providence, Rhode Island. I realized that I would have the opportunity to meet and be exposed to the general merchandise managers and CEOs of all the outstanding retailers associated with the Frederick Atkins Buying Office. Looking back, I made sure that the principals of these stores became aware of my performance at Gladdings with the hope that one day they might invite me to join their much larger stores.

I only recently realized when professors who read my book and request me to speak at different business schools about my experiences written in *Crossing Fifth Avenue* that many MBAs did not understand what it means to take advantage of a situation and would miss the opportunity when it came knocking at their door.

As I thought back, the first example of missed opportunities was when I was an adjunct professor at Columbia Business School in 1983. I offered the 39 MBAs in my class the opportunity to meet the CEO of any retail store that they desired. Much to my surprise, none took me up on my offer. The reason, at that time, was that most of the students were interested in Wall Street, not retailing. You would think retailers were not investing in expansion and other pursuits. I was greatly puzzled but put it down to another experience to learn from.

This was recently brought to mind when in my lectures at different business schools, I offered students the opportunity to contact me on "Ask the Author," a feature on my website (www.iraneimark.com) about any business questions regarding *Crossing Fifth Avenue* or to request the possibility of an introduction to an executive in their desired field. After each lecture this offer seemed to be well received. I went to my website waiting for the MBAs to contact me. About 10 out of the hundreds who have attended my lectures used my website to ask good questions. Only one asked for an introduction to Neiman Marcus.

I came to realize that my exposure to successful businesspeople, learning to be an opportunist at 17 years old, and taking advantage of the many opportunities advancing my business career from then on was five to eight years ahead of the MBAs, who would learn from experience only after they entered the workforce. They did not, to my regret, and unfortunately eventually theirs, recognize that by not taking the opportunity to connect with a seasoned, well-known, high-profile business executive, in order for them to develop an early network, when opportunity knocked, there was nobody there.

I got the impression that many of the MBAs undoubtedly felt that their brains alone would get them to where they wanted to go.

LESSONS LEARNED

It is what you know as well as who you know that gets results.

It never hurts and is very helpful to know people in high places.

Whenever possible, associate with successful business executives. Smart executives are always looking for talented people. It is better to be known than to be a face in the crowd.

As Russ Alan Prince and Lewis Schiff point out about Benjamin Franklin in their book *The Middle-Class Millionaire,* "Every turning point in the great man's life story required some deft combination of hard work and personal connections."

Lessons Learned from
the Great Depression

C AN A COMPARISON BE DRAWN between the Great Depression and the recent recession? Having lived through both, in my opinion, there is no comparison because the Great Depression was a disaster for everyone. There were bread lines all over New York, no employment insurance, and no other help for the 30 percent unemployed.

However, lessons can certainly be learned from the former to inform the latter. As one of the few retailers around today who began a career in retailing as far back as 1938, I am in somewhat of a position to show, as an example, how retailers survived the Great Depression then and to point out lessons to be learned by retailers today.

I can authenticate the beginning of my business career by recalling my very first job, delivering groceries and seeing the marvel of the large dirigible, *Hindenburg*, flying overhead on its way to its fiery demise at Lakehurst, New Jersey, on May 6, 1937. A year later, I was hired by Bonwit Teller to be a pageboy in its 721 Club.

I noticed immediately the contrast before I began work and after I entered the luxurious environment of Bonwit Teller. I also observed people in the subways and on the streets chugging along without a lot of optimism for the dismal immediate future; inside the opulent environment of Bonwit Teller was, to me, another world.

Bonwit Teller then recognized the potential business of the wealthy customer, even as the Depression continued, catering to this customer with all the elegance and service possible. It was this combination of the luxurious environment and professional management that proved to be the successful formula for Bonwit Teller and, I believe, for Saks Fifth Avenue, then under the management of Adam Gimbel.

Some department stores of the time—Namm's, Loeser's, and other large retailers—didn't make it through the Depression. But Bonwit Teller, Saks Fifth Avenue, Bergdorf Goodman, and many other family-owned stores with astute management came through just fine. (Bonwit Teller was owned by Atlas Corporation; however, its chairman, Floyd Odlum, and Hortense, whom Floyd installed as president, qualify it as family owned.)

The retailers' problems during the economic downturn in the twenty-first century came about through a combination of business strategies and decisions that were fraught with peril. In addition, most of the major retailers are now owned by public entities of one type or another, which must compete with each other by having their earnings reflect continued growth.

Compare this to years earlier when many if not most retailers were family owned. If a family-owned retailer had a poor year, the attitude was, next year we will try to do better. And they usually did.

The publicly owned retailers' sales grew enormously (largely) by opening branch stores rather than by increasing sales in their original stores. It was only natural that as the number of stores grew, inventories were geared to a larger market. In the process, many of the luxury-oriented branch stores diluted their luxury position, adding many achievers (new money) as their customers. When the economy deteriorated, the achievers dropped out of the luxury market. Additionally, these luxury retailers also lost some of their original core customers when they traded down to get a larger share of the market through their branch stores.

The disastrous iceberg that faced all the retailers, luxury and otherwise, was inventory management. Lost sales can always be recovered, expenses can always be lowered, but too much inventory, or being over-inventoried, is a burden many stores can't handle without destroying their profitability. Thus, calamity is a foregone conclusion.

LESSONS LEARNED

Nearly every retailer, those still in business and those recently departed after it was too late (e.g., Circuit City), realized they had overexpanded. In the process, those retailers over-inventoried to the point of financial disaster, in some cases worse than those of the Great Depression.

Many retailers eager to reduce their expenses made the cataclysmic error of drastically reducing their salespeople to the point that customers were left to look in vain for a salesperson to make a sale.

Helena Rubenstein and Elizabeth Arden: Another Lesson Learned

IN 1928, a year before the Great Depression, Helena Rubenstein, founding owner of one of the two giant luxury cosmetic houses of that time, sold her business to Lehman Brothers for more than 7 million dollars, a great amount of money, then and now.

The other luxury giant was Elizabeth Arden Cosmetics. Elizabeth Arden's strategy was to continue trading up during the Depression. As a result, Elizabeth Arden dominated the luxury beauty market.

During the Depression, with money scarce, women found that cosmetics could make them feel dressed up. This was a bonanza for the cosmetic companies who realized the upside potential.

These two ladies did.

Helena Rubenstein retired to Australia, where she followed reports of how during the Depression, Lehman Brothers traded Rubenstein Cosmetics down to popular prices and nearly destroyed the company. Madame Rubenstein returned to the States and was able to buy her company back, resumed her luxury program trading up, and caught up to the great success of her competitor, Elizabeth Arden.

Helena Rubenstein. (Roger Viollet/Getty Images.)

Elizabeth Arden. (Photo courtesy of Women's Wear Daily.*)*

Echoing this lesson more recently, in March 2010, *The New York Times* interviewed Donald Trump. Mr. Trump was asked, "What if your style of showy materialism has become passé?" His reply: "Great homes and apartments and things of great luxury will never be out of fashion. That's what people aspire to. It's a good thing, because it makes people work in order to attain that lifestyle."

Finding a Gold Mine in
the Lost Art of Customer Service

"CUSTOMERS SHOULD BE TREATED as valued assets to be treasured."

Let this thought roll around in your mind for a minute.

It is a statement too often overlooked in all types of businesses today. But there was a time, possibly as late as the early fifties, when storekeepers and other business executives were as aware of the need for superior customer service as they were to have desired merchandise on their shelves. These innovative merchants treated each and every customer as a "valued asset," knowing, through many years of experience, that with superior customer service, mainly with well-trained and dedicated sales staffs, there was a great potential available for that customer to spend beyond his or her initial intent.

In and around the fifties, "self-service" was developed. As I saw it, this started in the discount stores and gradually crept into department stores. Specialty stores soon followed, particularly those that featured apparel. Thus, we arrived at the point in department stores and specialty stores of floors of merchandise described as "Rack City."

Also about this time, many independent retailers were absorbed by public entities. Their major objective, among other priorities, was as it should be—the bottom line. However, in the process, a dedicated and experienced sales force often became one of the first casualties.

In addition, particularly as shopping malls developed, retailers came to the conclusion that because they were paying rent for their stores 24 hours a day seven days a week, they would keep their stores open seven days a week and every night as late as possible. That brought about what is called staggered hours. This meant spreading the minimum number of salespeople around in order to have "adequate coverage."

Because of the number of changes as outlined, slowly and bit by bit the professional, well-trained, and dedicated salesperson's role was reversed. They became sales clerks and cash register ringers (now credit-card swipers).

The result? The lost art of customer service.

Now let us talk about discovering and developing a gold mine. Good examples of businesses that learned and treat customers as valued assets are few and far between, but they are there and have prospered. Outstanding customer service has rewarded them as if they struck gold. Without naming them, you know who they are by your own experiences. You're surprised and then very pleased when an employee helping you performed at what you feel went beyond the call of duty. The strange part is that this type of customer service was considered natural in the recent past. Unfortunately, very many business executives either never learned nor understood the rewards of customer service and as a result have and will continue to suffer the consequence of limited sales and profits.

I have been asked if I can name one large national retailer that understands and is recognized for outstanding customer service.

Yes, there is one. Nordstrom.

It is a strange turn of events when Nordstrom is singled out as an exception in retailing as a retailer that is considered unique because it is dedicated to customer service. This should be the normal operating procedure—dedicated customer service from the CEO down to the sales clerk in all retail businesses today.

If large companies would devote major portions of their promotional budgets to develop dedicated and well-trained service personnel, instead of massive and expensive advertising campaigns, their returns would be the equivalent to the proverbial gold mine.

Consider these headlines and what may have kept them from ever being written:

Circuit City Stores criticized for laying off experienced salespeople. Wider than expected 3rd quarter loss. Stock went from $8.00 to $4.75. Now in Bankruptcy and liquidation (*Wall Street Journal*, November 21, 2007).

Sears to spend $50 million to $75 million advertising campaign (*The New York Times*, March 3, 2008).

What Is a Customer?

The following definition of "customer" has always been on my desk as a reminder to both my organization and myself:

- A customer is the most important person in our business.
- A customer is not dependent on us.
- We are dependent on the customer.
- A customer is not an interruption of our work.
- A customer is the purpose of it.
- A customer does a favor when he or she comes in.

- We are not doing customers a favor by waiting on them.
- A customer is part of our business, not an outsider.
- A customer is not just money in the cash register.
- A customer is a human being with feelings and deserves to be treated with respect.
- A customer is a person who comes to us with their needs, and wants; it is our job to fill them.
- Customers deserve the most courteous attention we can give them.
- A customer is the lifeblood of our and every business.
- A customer pays our salary.
- Without customers we would have to close up.
- Don't ever forget it.

Public Relations and
Turning a Business Around

ACCORDING TO PETER CUNEO, a veteran chief executive famous for turning businesses around, "It is much safer to revitalize a previously successful enterprise property than to assume the greater risk associated with creating new content." This was the approach used as a lever to bring back Bergdorf Goodman's international reputation and fashion image that it once had, but lost as the competition around it grew rapidly.

Everyone likes to see a favorite business that has fallen behind the times making a major effort to transform itself back to its glory days. My exposure to the magic of Bonwit Teller when it was the dominant fashion store on upper Fifth Avenue before it lost its way left me with the impression that there were an unlimited number of customers available to the retailer that became the dominant fashion store.

Studying little Henri Bendel across 57th Street, also merchandising its way to (for want of a better word) stardom, clicked in my mind. This was the formula required to bring Bergdorf Goodman back to and surpass everyone's modest expectations.

Building an organization to achieve these lofty ambitions was the hard part. Particularly with so many of the Bergdorf

Goodman buyers and merchandise managers seemingly insulated from being aware what it was that was moving the competition ahead while Bergdorf Goodman was, figuratively speaking, dead in the water.

Slowly but surely, the Bergdorf Goodman Fashion Office was reorganized, as was the Human Resource Department. Its coordinated efforts of selecting the newest and brightest talent brought about such a transformation that even the buyers leaving the organization recognized the need for change.

The next priority was to attract many of the top Italian, French, and American fashion designers to the store, who, in turn, would attract the new and well-to-do fashion-conscious customer. Developing an image of the smart and aggressive fashion store having talented fashion merchants with a "nose for news" was required.

Using advertising to create that image was tried unsuccessfully by Geraldine Stutz's predecessor, who came to Henri Bendel from Neiman Marcus. He felt that he could buy his way to a fashion reputation by copying Stanley Marcus, who got his reputation the hard way; he earned it. Geraldine Stutz proved this point without a shadow of doubt; using minimum advertising, she built an exciting, young, and very up-to-date fashion reputation. Customers came to her store in droves.

The strategy we found that worked most effectively to accomplish our objective was publicity.

Photographs from a *Women's Wear Daily* September 1977 issue prove the point. Bergdorf Goodman was featured in four different articles, replete with high-profile fashion names that no amount of advertising could buy. The photos and news articles featured the Fendi sisters, Geoffrey Beene, Aldo Pinto, the president of Krizia with Mariuccia Mandelli, and Bill Blass with Isabelle Leeds. PR of this kind made everyone aware that fashion excitement was happening at Bergdorf Goodman. The store was making its long way back to fashion dominance.

LESSONS LEARNED

It is most important in public relations to be associated and featured with the leaders of your field of endeavor, in order to reach your audience in the most positive terms possible. Good public relations will move a merchant to success. Bad or negative public relations will help bring a merchant to his or her demise.

Every business has its trade publications, too many to be named here. The leading retail publication, then and now, is *Women's Wear Daily. Women's Wear Daily*'s ability to spot rising trends helped Bergdorf Goodman to gain its place as a leading luxury fashion store enormously.

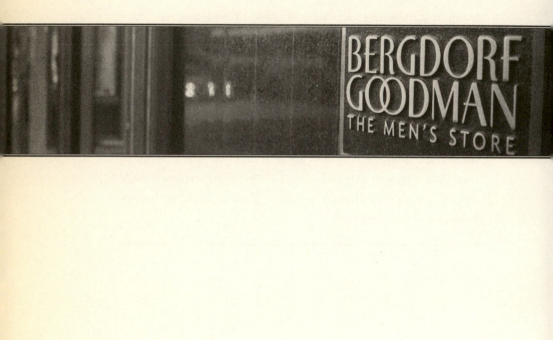

4

RETAIL COMMON SENSE

CONNECTING
WITH THE CUSTOMER

Newspaper Advertising:
Creating the Right Image

FROM MY BEGINNING as an office boy to Bill Holmes, advertising fascinated me. Possibly, it was the bright and very attractive young women who made up the department. I was smitten.

On my daily rounds, one of my first destination drop-offs was to chat with the copywriters. How I envied them. Their ability to look at a piece of merchandise and write about it and then to see it in *The New York Times* the next day was creative and magical.

Once in a while, the copywriters would show me merchandise and ask me to name it for copy in the ad. Imagine an 18-year-old seeing his words being used in the *Times*. I was impressed.

So much so that I attended evening advertising lectures given by Monroe Green, the advertising manager at *The New York Times* in the early forties, in order to prepare myself for a career in advertising. That was not to be. When I explained my advertising ambitions to my mentor, Bill Holmes, he explained the real money in retailing is in merchandising. If and when I became the head of a store, advertising would report to me. I would have the best of both worlds. He pointed me in that direction by promoting me to stock boy for the handbag department in the basement. From there, there was no other place to go than up.

His recommendation channeled my ambitions to being groomed to become a merchant. However, advertising all through my retail career has been if not my first love, then close to it.

Early in my career, I realized all retail stores, like people, have personalities. The personality of the stores was made up from a number of factors. The head of the store in all cases set the tone and personality of the store. Salespeople, location, physical plant, and merchandise carried are all reflections of the professionalism of the head or the owner. Take a look at the table "When Retail Stores Reflected Their Owners' Personalities." My descriptions may be arguable, but try to put an identity on many of the stores today.

Today many of the stores listed in the table, if still around, seem to spend an inordinate amount of money on the creativity and presentation for their display windows. And other large amounts of money are spent on newspaper advertising, showing clearance or sale merchandise day after day, mixed with fashion and item advertising. The contradiction to me is, as impressive as the display windows are to show the newest and the best that the store has to offer, window displays are seen only by traffic walking by, not necessarily by customers entering the store. Newspaper advertising reaches the four corners of the earth for all to see (for better or for worse). Add into the mix direct mail, magazine, Internet, and other emerging media of the twenty-first century and the possibilities for reaching your customers are virtually universal.

When Retail Stores Reflected Their Owners' Personalities

STORE	HEAD OF STORE	STORE REPUTATION
Bonwit Teller	Hortense Odlum	A Woman's Store
Saks Fifth Avenue	Adam Gimbel	An Elegant Store
Bergdorf Goodman	Edwin Goodman	A Couture Store
Lord & Taylor	Dorothy Shaver	The Newest Ideas
B. Altman & Co.	John Burke, Sr.	The Conservative Store
Gladdings	Frederick Aldred	A True Yankee Retailer
G. Fox & Co.	Beatrice F. Auerbach	Everybody's Favorite Store
Henri Bendel	Geraldine Stutz	Most Exciting Store
R.H. Macy & Co.	Jack Strauss	Greatest Values
Bloomingdales	Harold Krensky	The Store That Had Everything

I have always used two phrases taught to me many years ago that determine successful advertising strategies:

1. "Good advertising will speed a good merchant on to success. Good advertising will speed a poor merchant on to his demise." Sound merchandising is a must.

2. "Repetition is Reputation." Projecting the desired image over and over and over is the key for store recognition.

It would appear, if the display windows are used to show the best and newest, that same strategy projected in newspapers would help a store show its personality. I would add that the personality should be carried through the store, from salespeople to department displays.

The September 4, 1975, *Women's Wear Daily* article "New York Stores: Ad-ing It Up" tells the story of how six months after my arrival at Bergdorf Goodman, a new advertising format was presented for the first time in many years. The story also mentions that "B. Altman continued with the chatty-style ads it developed in 1973, as the first New York retailer to introduce a major departure from its previous look." At B. Altman we felt a chatty and witty approach was required in order to show the old customer and the new that something very current was taking place. Jane Trahey, a great copywriter from those days whose agency was responsible for many timeless slogans, gave B. Altman & Co. that needed boost.

Bergdorf Goodman's transformation from an old, dull, expensive, and intimidating store to a young, expensive, exciting, and intimidating store required a completely new image. Let me explain how that was done.

WOMEN'S WEAR DAILY, THURSDAY, SEPTEMBER 4, 1975

4

NEW YORK — One of the most competitive fashion retail markets in the world is New York City, where a strong advertising campaign provides a powerful advantage.

With the memory of disastrous fourth-quarter losses in 1974, stores have realized they can no longer rely on pat, formula, so-so advertising which may have worked in fatter spending times. The image each store presents to the buying world today must be au courant and decisive.

Accordingly, this fall is seeing several important format and look changes among key fashion retailers here. Two stores — Bergdorf Goodman and Lord & Taylor — will unveil new formats in this Sunday's New York Times. Bonwit Teller and Saks Fifth Avenue introduced their campaigns two weeks apart last month. Bloomingdale's premiered its campaign the last week in April. And B. Altman has continued with the chatty-style ads it developed two years ago as the first retailer to introduce a major departure from its previous look.

For the last several years, New York fashion retail advertising had been acquiring a certain sameness in look. Often, it was possible to remove the logo from each full-page ad in the Sunday Times and have difficulty in identifying the store from the ad style. Retail images were getting hazy. Ads were failing to zero in on the appropriate customer and, worse, to pique that customer's interest.

The new Altman's campaign featured illustrations with myriads of copy weaving along the length of the drawing, describing a trend, a new resource or a fresh look in almost irreverent, off-handed style, with selected words highlighted in boldface type. At the top of the ad was a provocative boldface headline, written to involve the customer directly.

It was a risky venture, since many readership studies have shown that a lot of ad copy turns off readers. But customers — and retail competitors — did read the ads and take notice. Other stores began to rethink their approaches.

After maintaining a low profile for many years, Bergdorf's will increase its traditional ads on page 3 and in the society section to a full-page ad in the family section on Sundays and at least one other day of the week, supplemented with smaller ads.

The page 3 small ad will remain. The new format has illustrations by Kenneth Paul Block and simple, straightforward captions indicating color, fabric, price and item description. The ad is framed by a dark rule which encircles the store logo, which has not changed.

"We are taking a stand. We feel we are the top specialty store in the country," said Ira Neimark, Bergdorf's president. "It is a very purist approach. We are saying, 'the best of whatever there is, is in this store.'

"The copy will be kept to a minimum," Neimark continued. "It should read like our very best salesperson explaining an item to a customer. We will talk about the merchandise, rather than how a customer will use it. And we will present only the merchandise which we feel indicates important trends." Neimark indicated the campaign is a strongly merchandise-oriented approach, "A pro talking to a pro, the way we see our customer and the store."

Unlike other retailers, Bergdorf's brought in outside advertising expertise. In April, the store hired Leber Katz Partners to develop the typeface and overall design. It was immediately decided to retain the distinctive logo and to abandon any clever copy approach.

Neimark, Neal Fox, vice-president and general merchandise manager and Dawn Mello, vice-president and director of fashion, decided on the approach. The advertising budget has been "restructured," according to Neimark; the budget remains the same with emphasis shifted from magazines to newspapers.

Advertising manager John Robinson said, "There will be some photography on appropriate items in the 300-line, smaller ads, but the strong emphasis is on fashion art." Block will draw all women's apparel ads, with the artist, Gaynor, commissioned for men's wear at present. Other artists might be added in the future.

After announcing to the trade, the media and its store personnel that its new campaign would include a new store logo as well as a copy and layout changes, Lord & Taylor has retrenched somewhat and returned to a stylized version of

Bergdorf Goodman's new ad face (top left) and old (far left); Bloomingdale's new campaign (top right); Lord & Taylor's new look (bottom right) and old ad (bottom left)

Ad-ing it up

familiar logo in ready-to-wear ads.

However, the Young New Yorker ads will ry the new logo, a lightface, all-capitalized lif, instead of the old script idea. Calligra- r A.C. Cypress refined the new logo with d & Taylor advertising director Carlo Ammi- , who also developed the new look. The new feature more active line drawings instead of sh illustrations, subheads and lighter faced, ner typography.

Ammirati indicated the new program was eloped within the regular store and budget, a ation existing in virtually all stores which re made major changes, according to the ex- tives interviewed.

"If we decided to go with photography, we'd re to hire an Irving Penn, an Avedon to get a tinctive enough look," said Ammirati. ong New York fashion stores, Lord & Taylor ploys perhaps the largest roster of free-lance ists: 15 of them assigned to various areas, in- ding home furnishings.

Since the new Bloomingdale's ad campaign oke just before Mother's Day, the format has n evolving from total use of sketches to the

on an item which is not high fashion."

Other than Massimo Vanielli, a graphic de- signer who designed the "Blooming type" type- face three years ago, the current campaign has been formulated with in-house talent.

The Saks Fifth Avenue campaign, which broke Aug. 17, uses a span of types, from cool, rather Wonder Woman figures (drawn by An- tonio and John Ansado) to photography. Doris Shaw, senior vice-president and corporate pro- motion director, said the store is maintaining the same proportions of drawings to photo- graphy in the new campaign: 75 percent to 25 percent.

"I would say the major change for us has been a more contemporary approach to the il- lustrations," said Ms. Shaw. "Our earlier draw- ings were softer. Now we want bolder women, a more interesting background and copy to reflect a more spirited woman."

The new ads have lighter, airier types, with more catchy headlines and subheads than be- fore. "We try for a conversational approach. No more typical, posed, arch drawings. We also are trying for an honest feeling. If it's just poetic, it

inscription on its Fifth Ave. facade. In addition, the new ads broke tradition because the Bonwit Teller signature no longer is part of the drawing nor must it be indicated in the headline.

The artwork, done by the same roster of art- ists, with the exception of Block, remains a com- bination line-and watercolor-wash style in a cleaner, uncluttered background. "You have to consider the psychic factor in clothes, which customers will be attracted to a certain style," said Tom Raney, marketing director. Raney and his staff, including Anny Queyroy, ad direc- tor, Ellen Burnie, art director and Carol Ezor, copy chief, pulled together the campaign.

"We're a fashion specialty store," Raney said. "Every three months, a majority of our merchandise is changed. If we don't have ex- citing ads, we're negating the every excitement of this place."

Bonwit's president George Baylis, said some might consider the new campaign not suf- ficiently revolutionary. "We haven't had an ex- treme change in artwork. We have no shock val- ue — a factor I don't consider a strength, by the way. I think the new concept has flexibility and

The new ad looks from Saks Fifth Avenue, Bonwit Teller and B. Altman.

lusion of some photography for certain home nishings. "We decided there is some mer- andise which cannot be shown in drawings," d Cathy Spellman, vice-president of commu- ations.

The format uses lots of white space with a ote as a headline. A recent directive from y chief Rex Berry to the 55 members of the y staff, has narrowed down the thrust of the adlines. Berry stresses informative head- es, zeroing in on a cleverly-written selling ssage to hurried readers.

Many of the ads are drawn by Michael Vol- acht and suggest dusky, shadowy figures, a d contrast to the white backgrounds. Other ists include Pedro Barrios, Jim Howard, Hei- Vuckovic and Betty Frazer. A new artist, anna Scribner, will begin doing men's wear s next week.

"We have been bothered by headlines which re too general and too fluffy," Ms. Spellman d. "The length of the head doesn't make any erence. At the same time, we can't turn off eone who wants a $29 suit by using a $3,000 rd in the copy. We try to get our drawings as se to the actual item as possible. And we must very careful that the faces represent the thes. We can't put a svelte, high-fashion face

isn't very valid," said Ms. Shaw.

Saks's president, Norman Wechsler, said the new campaign was developed "to make Saks more appealing and up-to-date. We've liked our previous campaign, but we must change — the way you change a wardrobe for fall. We some- times are thought of as a typical carriage trade store. We wanted to show we are very much au courant, without sacrificing our image of quali- ty and service."

Wechsler said the very image of the store projected in the ads could be, at once, the strongest and weakest point of the campaign: "We don't have that tremendous strong drive, the way A&S might do it. We aren't saying, 'Well, how many are we going to sell today?' But we do accomplish that in a low-key way, which is our strength."

Ms. Shaw said, "I feel the change came be- cause there is no more dogma about fashion. A store must show different attitudes, not a cookie-cutter feeling. We are trying for a poster effect, a major impact. Our old ads were becom- ing repetitious — frankly, I think all New York ads were."

Bonwit Teller introduced its new advertising Aug. 3 with a contemporary logo, which, coin- cidentally, more closely resembles the store's

presents the merchandise as the strong point. I asked for a refreshing, new look and the staff carried it out."

According to the Altman's hierarchy, the overwhelming reason for its ad change was to take away the feeling the store was a good home furnishings retailer with little fashion sense.

"We wanted to sell Altman's in its proper perspective, as a Fifth Ave. fashion store," said George Hanley, sales promotion director. "Coupled with that is the merchandise itself. Af- ter two years, I think the continuity of the ad program is its own strength and weakness. You have the similarity of white space, typeface, and copy approach. Yet this format can become bland. However, as a visual product, it's very successful. Take the store logo off and you still know it's Altman's."

Neimark was executive vice-president of Al- tman's before joining Bergdorf's and worked with Hanley and the staff on the campaign.

"Some have said they don't like to read all that copy, but many have written or contacted us to say they like the straightforward style," said Mary Irish, advertising manager, who writes the copy with the staff.

— BARBARA ETTORRE

"New York Stores: Ad-ing It Up," Women's Wear Daily, *September 4, 1975.*

(Reprint courtesy of Women's Wear Daily.*)*

First, we made merchandise changes, moving departments around in order to have the most wanted departments up front. For example, we moved cosmetics up to the front of the store from the rear. With a department move, we also developed women's sportswear, which had been weak, to be as strong as dresses. Moving departments around for the customer's satisfaction was one way to take on the old attitude of "Leave it; that is how it has always been."

Next, we decided which type of merchandise the department required to be brought to what a fashion-conscious customer expected. The quickest way to get the message of what was going on was, and still is, newspapers (notwithstanding the emerging media of the twenty-first century). Depending on the desired audience, *The New York Times* was the right media for Bergdorf Goodman. Public relations and direct mail, discussed earlier, are also excellent quick-response mechanisms. The Internet, a relative newcomer, will be discussed later.

Last, it is puzzling to me how major well-known retailers will spend untold fortunes on newspaper advertising, running full-page ads after full page, black-and-white and full-color, costing more than $50,000 a page. My puzzlement comes when the customer reads the ad, visits the store, and hopefully, for the customer and the store, attempts to buy whatever it was in the $50,000 advertisement but can't find a salesperson in sight.

It would seem to me, many of today's retailers are too far away from their selling floors to see what a terrible waste of money and reputation is going up in smoke, not in sales.

BERGDORF GOODMAN

NEW YORK got ready. The upcoming galas fell into place. The openings opened. The Metropolitan Museum of Art initiated what has become the Indian autumn of 1985 with its "India" exhibit, a precursor to Bergdorf's extracentennial main event in November. And the very tried to find one decent thing to wear. The answer? Bergdorf, where the sun never sets on our Spanish Creme Marfil marble floors and where Gianfranco Ferré's clothes calmly reside on two, the port in every autumn storm!

GIANFRANCO FERRÉ!!!
Day and Night
And Day!!

THOSE who really know are perfectly content this fall to leave color to the leaves. Ferré's gray suits suit us just fine, the jackets with lapels stitched to stand up, the skirts fitted and fluted. In coats, he plays with proportion, dropping the waists, then drawstringing the back. And he's even created a Ford for those urban autumn drives: The all wool, black empire dress, pictured at right, fall's simplest silhouette, all tailored stitchery, knit witchery, and very, very Gianfranco.

What else mattered last week? Sweaters mattered. And turtlenecks. Nobody has them in such profusion, beginning on the first floor by the 57th Street entrance, where the men's sweaters—pullover skis, a shoulder of Fair Isles—glow like the Northern Lights. On three, the sweater of the season for women: Turtleneck tapestry, all chenille intarsia on a field of white or burgundy. And Gloria Sachs's soft sweater sets, all gold and red and positively buttoned. Or our shawl collar pullover. The body orange. The waist a backgammon of color.

Valentino mattered, with his new boutique for men and woman on two, the clothes for both sleek and simmering, *That* Valentino. Always cutting it close.

And evening mattered. The order of the night? Dresses that hug you the way you always told your husband to do it. Like he means it. Like Anthony Price's black velvet strapless, slit up the back with a bow as big as a bustle. On four. And like the short and long of Fabrice, also on four. This fall, shape, for him, is everything, his necklines taking every plunge you ever dreamed of.

After Such Finery
What Forgiveness?

NONE, of course. Only more finery, like Bergdorf's newest shirts, in the finest cotton, with stitched, pleated necklines, developed by B.G.'s own buyers with the foremost international tailors. Or our printed silk tunics from England, a field of foulard with rhinestone buttons. All on three.

Almost nothing mattered more, however, than the return of Pat, our doorman, to his post on our 58th Street door. Now you'll revolve through the door without incident *on your way to* your hair appointment at the Sergio Valente beauty center on 7, our gift floor, all of which should put you in fine shape before you meet, yes that's right, Olivier Echaudemaison, the inimitable French makeup artist who's been waiting for you at the Estée Lauder counter. So what took you so long? B.G. knows. You were waiting for Pat.

On the Plaza in New York

Bergdorf Goodman advertisement in The New York Times *strategically placed beside a column covering the latest fashions at Bergdorf Goodman. (Reprint courtesy of* The New York Times.)

LESSONS LEARNED

Many of the merchants listed in the table "How Retail Stores Reflected Their Owners' Personalities" taught me the best way to attract customers to their stores was strive to offer new and exciting merchandise every day of the year—and if not every day, as often as possible.

Markdown and clearance merchandise should be the smallest part of the store's daily offering. This merchandise should be removed with the least amount of advertising and the most amount of markdown to accomplish that objective.

Good advertising will speed a good merchant on to success. Good advertising will also speed a poor merchant on to his demise.

Customer Loyalty

USTOMER LOYALTY IS A PHRASE not commonly used today by either retail CEOs or their customers. Here, too, it is necessary to go back a good number of years when retailers considered this concept a critically important part of their business strategy.

The subjects for this book address the positive and exciting aspects of the growth of the fashion industry but also, unfortunately, the decline of customer service. This decline brought about the loss of customer loyalty as practiced so successfully many years ago.

To properly present customer loyalty as the bedrock of smart retailing, through the book, I went back and traced my career from the very beginning to illustrate how the concept became part of my retail religion. My very first exposure to gain customer loyalty was in 1938, convincingly demonstrated, even during the Great Depression. My exposure to Bonwit Teller's commitment to customer service made an unforgettable impression on my young mind.

The doorman at the store's Fifth Avenue entrance as well as the doorman on 56th Street were both to welcome customers by name whenever possible. A white-gloved parking service attendant whisked the customer's car away and parked it until called for. Numerous salespeople were trained to treat customers as guests in their home. Service managers made sure those customers were properly taken care of, and, of course, saw that sales were made. Weekly lunches were held with customers of the store by the president of Bonwit Teller to determine their likes and dislikes. Their customers loved their store.

Fast-forward 21 years later to G.Fox & Co.'s Beatrice Fox Auerbach. There is no question in my mind that this store president/owner understood and practiced the need for customer loyalty better than most anyone I have met before or after. The possible exception was Stanley Marcus of Neiman Marcus. An aside: In the mid-sixties, I attended a meeting of the National Retail Dry Goods Associates (now the National Retail Federation, or NRF). When Beatrice Fox Auerbach arrived, the hundreds of retail executives stood and applauded the lady as recognition of the great merchant that she was. G. Fox & Co. was without a doubt everyone's favorite store and engendered unmatched customer loyalty. It was one of the largest department stores north of New York City and south of Boston (in Hartford, Connecticut). The assortment of merchandise from the bargain basement up to the 11th floor was as completely well stocked as humanly possible. This was due to Beatrice Auerbach's continued very strict merchandising discipline and diligence.

The store was open only five days a week, a custom left over from the era of World War II. Hartford was a major insurance-company city and the insurance company employees worked five days a week, Monday through Friday. To attract these employees, retailers matched the five-day workweek by opening their doors Tuesday through Saturday. This allowed everyone's favorite salesperson to be available for the customer's convenience, assuring the sale. There were no bean-counter tricks such as staggered sales help to lower selling costs, which only encouraged staggered sales.

Every customer knew if for any reason he or she was dissatisfied with any aspect in Mrs. Auerbach's store, its owner could be reached and the problem would *always* be resolved to the customer's satisfaction. This CEO understood her customers and what it took to satisfy them as she would want to be satisfied herself.

Fast-forward again to today.

There is no question that the proliferation of so-called regular-priced retail stores, discount stores, and specialty store retail chains makes it impossible for the CEO to put his or her imprint on their organization when one store was the rule rather than the exception. Unfortunately, these stores in the past 25 years or so frequently advertise off-price sales, clearance sales, special sale days, or whatever in order to attract customers to their stores. They are not unlike barkers at the circus, each claiming their price offering is better than their neighbors or competitors.

Not too many years ago, regular-priced retailers had their first major fall sale on the Friday after Thanksgiving (erroneously named Black Friday). The month of December was devoted to selling regular-priced holiday merchandise. The week between Christmas and New Year's Day was the next legitimate sales bonanza. This approach seemed to work quite well until some retailers began running sales of off-price merchandise so frequently that customers went from store to store looking for the best bargains. Forget customer loyalty.

Whoever had the biggest markdown drew the most customers. In the process, many stores, for the most part, lost their original identity as well as their customers' loyalty.

The reader will note, earlier in this book I mentioned earning customer loyalty was, for me, like religion. It must be practiced every day.

Today I am afraid that many CEOs have lost the connection with their customers. They have, due to multiple stores, delegated what I consider their responsibilities to staff after staff. If the reader feels that I am being unduly critical, please walk from store to store. What you will find in most cases are few salespeople, many not too well trained, at best understanding how to make one sale but surely not two.

The solution? Every CEO should delegate at least one day out of his or her very busy schedule to walk one of his or her stores (I prefer unannounced). This is called earning their MBWA degree (Management By Walking Around), an expression I first heard many years ago.

Merchants know and understand their customers' wants and requirements; financial people, I have observed over many years, do not.

A walking tour answers the following questions:

- Are there salespeople available for the customers?
- Are the salespeople dressed appropriately, representing how the CEO sees his or her store?
- Are salespeople busy talking with each other or talking on their cell phones instead of paying attention to customers who pay the store's bills, including their own salaries?

Every salesperson must be indoctrinated with the CEO's retail philosophy, if there is one (and there should be).

LESSONS LEARNED

As American retailers continue to expand nationally and even internationally, customer loyalty must be built into the store just as surely as bricks and mortar, not as an afterthought.

Online retailing, slowly but surely, in many cases (not all) is developing customer loyalty, which in many cases will make the average young customer gravitate away from many retailers who think self-service is the answer to building successful businesses.

The Real Retailers: A Social History

W HEN I ACCEPTED the position of the ready-to-wear merchandise manager at Gladdings in Providence, Rhode Island, I was not aware that Gladdings belonged to the Frederick Atkins Buying Office. This was another stroke of very good luck in my young career.

Many small privately owned (family) retailers of that time paid fees to independent buying offices, located in New York, for their buying expertise. These retailers located around the country required the knowledge of the New York–based buyers to direct their store buyers to the proper manufacturers to purchase the desired merchandise to have in their stores.

The larger retailers such as Bloomingdales in New York; Lazarus in Columbus, Ohio; Filene's in Boston; and Abraham & Strauss in Brooklyn belonged to major retail entities such as Federated Department Stores. The other major store group at the time was May Department Stores, which owned stores such as Famous Barr in St. Louis, Kaufmann's in Pittsburgh, Hecht Co. in Baltimore, and Meier & Frank in Portland, Oregon, to name a few. Both Federated and May Co. had their own large buying organizations here in this country as well as abroad. Frederick Atkins Inc. was a buying office owned by privately owned independent retailers. These retailers were preeminent in their communities. The Atkins office was located in New York City. The office's function was to supply the member stores with up-to-date buying information. The stores were located in cities distant from each other, as far as from Boston to San Diego and nearly every state in between. Joining Gladding in Providence was my introduction to many of these retailers whose families started their stores from, in many case, wagons going west or as mere storefronts in their cities. Many of these stores grew to become the most influential retailers in their cities.

My good fortune was to be exposed to many of the executives from these stores; this formed and guided my early career. It led me to the belief that I too one day would be the CEO of a store of my choice. The stories of Bill Holmes at Bonwit Teller, Leonard Johnson at Gladdings, Beatrice Fox Auerbach at G. Fox & Co., and Randy Stambaugh and Jack Burke at B. Altman & Co. have been covered. In addition, meeting a number of CEOs and merchandising executives from the Atkins Stores gave me the opportunity to learn from long-established and successful retailers.

One of my first challenges was to determine the correct price levels for the successful merchandising of Gladdings men's and women's apparel. My luck continued, by meeting Martin Kohn, the president of Hochschild Kohn in Baltimore. I was invited by him to meet his ready-to-wear merchandise manager, Sigmund Lampell, to study their price lines. Edwin Hyde, the president of Miller & Rhoads in Richmond, Virginia, invited me to learn from Bill Fritz, his ready-to-wear manager. Finally in my quest, I met Ludwig (Wig) Amtmann. He was the general merchandise manager of Woodward & Lothrop, in Washington, D.C. I got to know Wig quite well and found him to be a very wise counselor in my early retail career. All three executives were mature, successful merchants with long years of experience. I was very fortunate that they shared their collective knowledge with me, which enabled me to guide my first retail strategy to success.

About this time, I learned that Elmer Stevens, the president of Charles A. Stevens & Co. in Chicago, another Atkins store, had developed an approach to unit merchandising that I was trying to develop for my merchandising strategy. I got on another plane, this time to Chicago, after visiting Baltimore, Richmond, and Washington to learn more.

Elmer Stevens was an elderly man who startlingly resembled President Dwight D. Eisenhower. When I entered his office at 8:00 a.m. as requested, he was already busy reviewing his unit inventory reports in order to determine, department by department, which slow-moving merchandise was destined to be marked down and which fast-moving merchandise was to be reordered. I had found another kindred spirit. Here too I adopted some of Elmer Stevens's ideas and incorporated them into my merchandising procedures. I was able to use this procedure very successfully for the rest of my retail career.

My definition of the "Real Retailers" stemmed from my many years of exposure to these retailers, who were all successful merchants. They grew up in their family businesses learning how to properly service customers, make profits, and build businesses and careers. They knew how to run their stores from the bottom up. The merchants in the family ran the stores. The financial people in the stores, family or otherwise, were in the back office. Unfortunately, today in many if not most cases, the financial people have taken over, and even though retailers have grown tremendously, their customers have suffered, not knowing the enjoyment of shopping during the time of the Real Retailers.

As Martin Kohn wrote in his brief history of Hochschild Kohn & Co., "I must confess that I miss the old store with its stress on quality, service, and warmth."

As with all businesses, the evolution of retailing from the Real Retailers with their stores that stressed quality, service, and warmth has led to the giants. They have proven, in many cases, that size alone is not the formula for success. The changing shopping habits of customers and social mores will dictate the long-range future for retailing.

LESSON LEARNED

Shopping is a very personal experience. Customers must be treated as valued assets, to be treated as individuals who require attention and interest for their shopping needs, not treated as a crowd of people who, if they look hard enough, may find what they want to buy.

The Benevolent Dictator

IN "THE REAL RETAILERS: A SOCIAL HISTORY,"
I recalled the names of all the professional retailers
whom I had the good fortune to know and work with
over many years. Each in his own way left a mark of
professionalism on me that I tried to incorporate into my retail
philosophy and life in general.

The following *Women's Wear Daily* article by David Moin,
"Bergdorf's Benevolent Dictator," which ran on September 30,
1991, explains some of the major steps I used to bring Bergdorf
Goodman to its leadership in luxury fashion merchandising:

"You have to keep pounding away and away and away again, and eventually they get it."

That's Ira Neimark, chairman and chief executive officer of Bergdorf Goodman, discussing how he manages his staff. Calling himself "a benevolent dictator," Neimark—who retires in February after 16 years at the store—describes life at Bergdorf's this way: "We can fight like families, but we work like a team."

He's got a tough, paternalistic credo, and a routine that brings the six-foot, one-inch, 69-year-old merchant bounding through the store with the energy of someone half his age, telling staff to put mannequins and markdown racks in their proper place, replace a burned-out lightbulb or pick up a fallen pricetag. He's blunt, meticulous and patrols his store like a traffic cop—but not without a coat of charm.

"When he says he wants something done, he wants it done at that moment—not the next day," says Barry Kieselstein-Cord, the fine jewelry designer. "With Ira, you always know where you stand."

Others know him as a retail activist. As Tiffany's chairman William Chaney says, Neimark has been "adamant, outspoken and caring about Bergdorf's and the Fifth Avenue district."

These are among the characteristics that helped Neimark establish Bergdorf Goodman as one of the most exclusive fashion stores in the world, with many of the globe's highest caliber and most expensive designers.

Yet, even upscale businesses have been squeezed by the recession, and Bergdorf's is no exception. In figures published as recently as Friday, Bergdorf's reported that for the year ended July 27, it suffered an 82.1 per-cent slide in operating profits on a 6.1 percent sales gain. A few days earlier, Neimark had acknowledged that the results would be disappointing but said Bergdorf's must "ride out" the weak economy and not change its focus.

"For the short term," he said, "I see Bergdorf's as a $200 million women's business." He predicted the men's store will exceed $50 million in another year, adding, "There's a possibility of opening another men's store."

He said the men's business made its projection of $40 million in sales for the last fiscal year, but admitted gross margins could have been better.

In a good economy, he said, the men's store would have been "outstanding."

Neimark brought to Bergdorf's "a strategy that went beyond just getting lines," says Dawn Mello, former president and fashion director, now executive vice president and creative director with Gucci. "It involved adjacencies, advertising and publicity."

It also involves a hard stance on markdowns, which are not advertised.

"The first markdown is your best markdown," explains Neimark. "Take it fast, move it fast. Every buyer must every week determine the 12 best-selling and 12 slowest selling items. If it's not selling within 30 days, look at it carefully and move it out. We believe the customer is entitled to fresh, new assortments. We rarely run a clearance, maybe one around Christmas."

Along with that, Neimark has a management philosophy based on homespun homilies. He tells of an old sign hanging in his garage that reads, "Wipe your shoes before you come into this house," and says, "You have to run a store as you would your home. There are some stores where there are peddlers in the lobby—I won't tell you which ones. I've fought to get the peddlers off the streets."

Neimark has been in retailing for 53 years and believes in control from the top. He insists key meetings with designers be held on a "principal-to-principal" level and says buyers are the "instruments to carry out the details."

He thinks a "strong fashion office" is important but said the store must reflect what the CEO believes in.

Neimark says he hasn't eased up on the reins of command one bit, although he seems ready to enter a new phase of life. He recently bought himself a Jaguar convertible, and says he'll be spending more time with his wife, Jackie, whom he met in 1952 on a blind date and married a year later.

He'll also spend more time with his two married daughters and two grandchildren.

He's bemused when people ask him, "What are you going to do?"

He points out that he plays golf at least once a week and sails his 27-foot sloop, which is moored next to a nineteenth-century mill in Rye, New York, near his home in Harrison. He also fishes for bass near his home, hunts pheasant, and enjoys taking photographs when traveling. A favorite retreat is Nassau in the Bahamas.

He also finds tranquility taking off his shoes and eating sushi in a private room in a Japanese restaurant—or crab cakes at The Four Seasons. He's a man who knows the good life. . . .

In some ways, Neimark's mission at Bergdorf's is completed. He's transformed the store into perhaps the most exclusive fashion store in the country; opened a new business, Bergdorf Goodman Men, and was instrumental in selecting his successor, Burt Tansky, who became vice chairman in January and takes over as CEO in February.

All of this makes retirement palatable and logical.

"After working full-time for more than 50 years, I'm looking forward to taking off my tight shoes, so to speak," Neimark says.

Tansky fits Neimark's criteria for a good merchant.

"The first thing is how well you work with people," Neimark says. "You have to be accepted by your people. Secondly, is he a good merchant? That means does he know how to make a profit with fashion merchandise? And third, how good an eye does he have?"

"I identified him [Tansky] to the Neiman Marcus Group. I'm thrilled with him. I think after a year at Bergdorf's, you begin to understand Bergdorf's is a different type of operation.

"I'd like to maintain a relationship to the fashion business," Neimark adds, explaining that he plans to be a consultant to retailers on a selective basis. A previous arrangement to be a consultant with General Cinema—which owns Bergdorf's, Neiman Marcus and Contempo Casuals—has been dropped because Neimark felt there might be a conflict of interest. He says he won't maintain an office in New York, but still continues his love affair with the Fifth Avenue–57th Street area.

That began in 1938, when he took his first retail job, at Bonwit Teller. It was a Christmas job as a page in the store's 721

Club for men, a shop offering a sampling of the store's best items.

"The mood was Cole Porter, we were coming out of the Depression and there were attractive women, wealthy men and the store looked great," he recalls. "It was the tip of the fashion world."

His father wanted him to follow in his footsteps as a lawyer, but Bonwit's "was the place for me," he says. "I was very impressionable at 18."

William Holmes, president of Bonwit's at the time and a mentor, taught him that the two most important segments in the business were the market and the salespeople.

"If you have them on your side, you can do anything," Neimark says. "Because of that, I made it a point of being in the market at least one day a week. If you go through the store you can get to know most of the salespeople by name and they can give you a better understanding and an awful lot of feedback."

Last week, on one of his store patrols, he said salespeople were requesting more in-depth assortments.

"We have the styles and we are still running a very strong business," he says, although the salespeople convinced him, as he puts it, to start studying the individual orders closer.

After Bonwit's, Neimark joined Gladdings in Providence, R.I., then G. Fox in Hartford, Conn., where he worked under Beatrice Fox Auerbach, head of the store, and another mentor.

"She taught me the store should be as clean as your home. She would walk through the store and ask people to move the furniture so she could check for dust. She was very critical of her own operation. She gave me a philosophy I still use today: 'Don't tell me what's right; I know what's right. Tell me what's wrong.'"

He returned to New York, joining B. Altman's, where he was an executive vice president and general merchandise manager, and moved to Bergdorf's in 1975 as president and CEO.

Phil Hawley, chairman of Carter Hawley Hale, which owned Bergdorf's at the time, was the man who brought in Neimark and gave him the mandate to make Bergdorf's a fashion force.

"He backed me all the way," Neimark says. "It was an old, dull, expensive and intimidating store. My job was to make it young, exciting, expensive and intimidating. The talk of fashion at the time was Armani and YSL. Bendel's and Bloomingdale's were the hot stores."

Fendi was the first major Italian designer Neimark convinced to sell to Bergdorf's, in 1977. From then on, Neimark's strategy for Bergdorf's blossomed.

"I told [the five Fendi sisters] that we had a commitment to make Bergdorf's the best fashion store in the world,' Neimark recalls. "We were not interested in a quick fix. We were interested in the best names in the industry, providing a proper showcase, and presenting merchandise in a very fashionable manner."

According to Mello, the Fendis thought selling Bergdorf's would be a "crapshoot," yet "they liked us" and ended up getting practically half the main floor. Bergdorf's was setting an example.

It became a habit for Neimark, Mello and the team to lug bottles of champagne to parties after fashion shows in designers' showrooms. Soon they started winning over others. Krizia and Giorgio Armani followed Fendi.

In the eighties, however, Neimark dropped Fendi. Later, Hermès ready-to-wear was also dropped. In both cases, it was because the firms widened distribution beyond Neimark's tolerance.

"We fight for maintaining our marketing of exclusives or semi-exclusives," he says. "If a designer is in only one or two stores [in New York], we can build a shop. And if the merchandise is exclusive, it goes in the windows."

In the late seventies, Neimark wanted Rive Gauche by Yves Saint Laurent, which was being sold at

Saks and Bloomingdale's. Neimark used a roundabout method, and bought the couture. The decision reportedly didn't make money. However, Pierre Berge, chairman of YSL, was impressed, and it led to the building process for YSL at Bergdorf's. Mello adds that the couture "caused a great deal of conversation."

Neimark was elevated to chairman in 1983, and continued his efforts to bring in the best designers. He told Calvin Klein in 1986 that Bergdorf's would build him a shop and, in return, Klein gave Bergdorf's the pick of the litter from his collection—the exclusive right to about 20 styles.

Other stores were rocked by the arrangement, and Klein was in the awkward position of having to tell them about it right after showing his collection. Neimark was there.

"It made Mel Jacobs [CEO of Saks Fifth Avenue] unhappy," Neimark remembers. "So Klein told Mel, 'Look I can only make so many pieces and Bergdorf's is the right size.' I think Calvin chose a good way out."

For Neimark, it capped the most exciting and challenging period of his career.

"Bloomingdale's, Saks and Bendel's," says Neimark. "To be able to break into that group, it was tough."

Reprinted with permission from Women's Wear Daily.

Focus Groups and Other Myths

M Y CAREER at Bergdorf Goodman began long before focus groups, or at least before I became aware of them and what they were supposed to accomplish.

Fortunately, with my early experiences and exposure to well-to-do customers at Bonwit Teller and how they wanted to be treated and served, it was not very difficult to determine the strategy to be used. We set out transforming Bergdorf Goodman from an old, dull, expensive, and intimidating store to a young, exciting, expensive, and intimidating store. These targeted customers are the people who went to the best restaurants, best hotels, and best resorts and belonged to the best clubs.

Once the personality of the customer was determined, the merchandise content and all the services of the store were to be linked to that customer. Again, as previously mentioned, a fashion director's office was established to select the newest and most exciting collections of merchandise in the European and American markets to be carried in the store.

The merchandising organization was to be made up of the savviest group of buyers who would understand, appreciate, and follow the fashion office's direction and supervision.

The mechanics of how much to buy and when to buy was the function of the divisional merchandise managers. It was not their function to determine what to buy. What to buy was the fashion office's responsibility.

Obviously, at this point, other fashion functions came into play. Advertising, fashion shows, Fifth Avenue display windows, interior displays, public relations events, and press releases: These were all coordinated by the Fashion Office.

The financial division's responsibility was to see to the financing of the divisions as described above. Its most important function was to manage the expenses of the growing sales to a reasonable, if not a higher, profit and better-than-average return on investment.

Last but far from the least came personnel and operations. These two functions were tied together, since it was the responsibility of the personnel department to hire the type of salespeople who would relate to the targeted customers. Sales training came under the operations office. No matter what, salespeople were to treat customers with the same courtesy as guests in their own home. If they couldn't meet that requirement or were found not to practice that rule, they were recommended to work elsewhere, preferably for our competition.

With all of the above in place, slowly but surely, Bergdorf Goodman awakened from its long slumber to once again gain its rightful place as one of the leading fashion stores in America, as well as reflecting its great luxury specialty store reputation around the world.

Planning and opening Bergdorf Goodman's Men's Store was slated for the right opportunity at the right place and arguably at the right time. The store was to open in September 1990. Unfortunately, a recession started in July of that year, and the store did not make its initial projections. The powers-that-be were alarmed and felt that with all of the above strategies in place, a focus group was in order.

When I questioned this plan, I was told this was a very professional group, and I am sure they were. I was also told the focus group would select men who would presumably shop at Bergdorf's Men's Store, and they were to be paid $100 for their participation. I laughed then, and I must say, when I think about it, I laugh today. I marveled at the focus group not being aware of the customer that we were aiming for. That customer would leave $100 as a tip at any good restaurant without a second thought.

The expression MBWA, Management By Walking Around, is as good a strategy today as it was when I first heard it many years ago. The dearth of senior management, from CEOs on down, who walk through their stores on a regular basis is a failure. Not listening, not asking questions, and not watching their salespeople's skills or lack of attention to customers and customer reactions are other shortcomings.

Management using focus groups to do their thinking for them reminds me of another old New England expression: "It is like kissing a girl through a screen door."

LESSON LEARNED

There is no question, in any business, that it is imperative to know as much as possible about your present and potential customer. Focus groups, like political pollsters, must ask the right questions from the right people in order to get the right answers; otherwise, the wrong answers are arrived at, furthering the confusion. The focus group should be your own customers, who, more than anyone, know what they like about your business and what they do not like.

CUSTOMER SERVICE MEANS BUSINESS

"Because That's Where the Money Is"

A S I HAVE MENTIONED BEFORE, salesmanship seems to be a lost art. All retailers bemoan the fact when a snowstorm, or other inclement weather, causes customers to stay home instead of shopping, it will ruin their sales. I am reminded of a wonderful retail story that I heard many years ago, so long ago that I may have the wrong names. However, whenever the weather turned bad for me, I thought about it.

Mr. Strawbridge or Mr. Clothier was going to a dinner party, and a snowstorm was forecast for the next day. When one of the great retailers complained to his wife that the storm would ruin his business, his wife responded, "Many years ago we had a small store in downtown Philadelphia. It has snowed and stormed for over 50 years. We now have a store that covers a whole city block. It would seem to me, something other than the weather had something to do with that."

One of the key ingredients she was referring to was in a book I read recently, *Golf and the Art of Customer Service*, by brothers Michael and Robert Reiss. This book explains more clearly than most the importance of customer service contributing to shareholder value:

Customer service means business. A recent JD Powers five-year study revealed that organizations that improved customer service increased shareholder value by 52 percent, while those organizations whose service declined lost 28 percent of their value. If you want to improve your organization's performance, you must start with the customer experience.

Customer experience has many different approaches. The one that has always appealed to me as the most important is salesmanship. Salesmanship starts before the customer enters the store. Is the store in a convenient location for the customer? Is the store easy to reach? If parking is required, is it easy, handy, courteous, and welcoming? If the store has display windows, do the windows reflect the store's personality? Does the advertising reflect the store's true identity?

Entering the store is as important as a guest entering your home. A guest is never told, "The closet for your coat is over there." Imagine the host not greeting the guest by saying hello, which happens in nearly every type of store a customer enters today, from luxury to mass volume.

Many years ago, to ensure good customer service, there was a level of management known as the floor manager. This person's most important responsibility was to be sure customers were being taken care of. Why? As the bank robber Willie Sutton said, "Because that's where the money is."

The floor manager was in command of the selling floor. A qualified salesperson was there to make the sale happen.

Volume retailers can learn a great deal from the Apple stores. No matter which Apple store a customer enters, there are salespeople. All know their products, as well as their role as professional salespeople. They are not only polite and knowledgeable but also extremely helpful.

In one of the last mass-marketing stores I recently visited, I asked the manager, who finally came to the selling floor (where the business is done), "Where are your salespeople?" He said, with a straight but sad expression on his face, "When business went bad, they let all the salespeople go."

Good salespeople are made, not born. When retailers realize it is more important to have more trained salespeople on the selling floor to take care of customers instead of more security people, they will realize what the great merchant's wife from Philadelphia meant when she told her husband why their store now covered a whole city block.

LESSON LEARNED

Customers are human beings and appreciate being helped, whether it means showing them where the merchandise they are looking for is located or explaining what it will do for them. Anything that helps to make the shopping experience enjoyable will prove to be profitable. Much better than hoping for good weather.

What Goes Around Comes Around

ARLIER IN THIS BOOK I wrote about how until about the sixties many department stores had "Bargain Basements," which they eventually, except for Filene's Basement, gave up as a gift to the newly emerging discount stores.

I refer to this retail evolution in my book *Crossing Fifth Avenue to Bergdorf Goodman* by describing how I brought the discount stores' threat to the attention of the principals of the approximately 70 privately owned department and specialty stores that belonged to the buying office Frederick Atkins, Inc. The audience of my distinguished colleagues received my message poorly and with skepticism. All these stores, except for Dillard's Department Stores, went out of business during the next 10 to 20 years.

It took about another 25 years for the fashion designers to realize that opening their own "closeout stores" in shopping malls was a bonanza. Not only were the designers able to sell the over-cuts and returns from retailers at a profit but they also were able to produce tremendous quantities of lower-quality, lower-priced designer-label merchandise at very satisfactory profits. Customers flocked to these stores, many with the delusion that they were buying original designer merchandise at great discounts.

It took traditional retailers close to 52 years later to realize they too could get back into the lost "Bargain Basements" by opening many closeout stores. Luxury retailers began to open their own larger "closeout stores"; these include Neiman Marcus's "Last Call," Saks Fifth Avenue's "Off Fifth," and "Nordstrom's Rack." Today, every retailer has found, as the older retailers knew, lower-income customers needed bargains, and higher-income customers enjoyed them. Nearly every large retailer, department, or specialty store has opened or will open lower-price merchandise stores with their prestigious name as the legitimacy for the merchandise carried.

For those stores that have not taken this road, sale merchandise is offered on a daily basis, making customers wonder when the regular-priced merchandise will go on sale.

LESSON LEARNED

To be a successful retailer, it is imperative to be aware of customers' wants and needs. Those retailers who ignored the tremendous success of discount stores disappeared. Successful retailers today package their discount merchandise with attractive stores, satisfying the customer who needs a bargain and the customer who enjoys having one.

Luxury-Brand Customers

ALL THROUGH MY RETAIL CAREER, going as far back to before World War II up to the present, during social, political, economic, and national upheavals, the same question has been asked: "How will this affect our business?" The answer over the years depended on the income level of the customer of the store that I was involved with at that time.

During the Great Depression, Bonwit Teller, the top fashion store in New York at that time, suffered somewhat, as did all the luxury retailers, for a number of years following that dismal economic period. Needless to say, retailers at lower-price levels suffered even more. With my beginning at Bonwit Teller near the end of the Depression, as mentioned earlier, I realized that the very wealthy arrived every day in their chauffeur-driven limousines. They drove up in numbers large enough to keep me busy all day long. And those driving their own cars kept the five or six parking attendants very busy as well. The luxury business continued to thrive.

A year later, as the office boy to Bill Holmes, one of my assignments was to shop and observe the number of customers the other luxury stores drew. Mr. Holmes considered his main competition Saks Fifth Avenue and the great children's store Best & Co. I recall these stores also enthralled me with their elegance and their attractive customers. I was not expert enough at the time to determine Saks or Best's sales figures, but I was aware enough to report back, "They looked busy."

In my involvement over the years with more popular-priced stores—James McCreery & Co., Gladdings, G. Fox & Co., Brown Thompson, and B. Altman & Co.—I noticed that, not surprisingly, financial and economic downturns had a stronger negative effect on these businesses than higher-end stores. Later when I was offered the position of CEO at Bergdorf Goodman, my experience at Bonwit Teller many years earlier helped make my decision easier. My more recent work at upper-medium-priced stores such as G. Fox and B. Altman also greatly influenced my decision. The luxury market for many reasons always appealed to me. The fact that wealthy customers simply are the least affected in an economic downturn is not the only reason for the appeal, but it is an important one.

It wasn't necessary for me to ask a business consultant whether I should accept the job as CEO of Bergdorf Goodman with its great growth potential. The luxury customer was there—if I employed the lessons learned many years earlier at Bonwit Teller.

In answer to more recently asked questions about how the luxury market is reacting to all of the negative financial, economic, and international problems at the start of the second decade of the twenty-first century, once again history repeats itself with two favorable major developments that did not exist in years past. First, in this country there are many more luxury-brand customers in the market willing to spend whatever it takes to satisfy their desires. Second, there are today more luxury brands in business than ever before in history to satisfy these desires, both domestically and internationally. My exposure to these companies as the former CEO of Bergdorf Goodman and as a director of Hermès of Paris indicates that, as in the past, the luxury-buying public at the high end are not changing their buying habits. However, the marginal luxury customer is reducing their buying, affecting the retailers who sell middle, upper-middle, and luxury merchandise. The truly luxury retailer who sells to the top of the luxury market has less difficulty riding out a negative financial climate.

LESSONS LEARNED

During any economic uncertainty, high-income customers will continue to purchase luxury merchandise in an elegant environment.

Lower-income (aspiring) customers will drop out of the luxury market until the economy recovers.

Style, Luxury, Quality, and Value

Style

I have been asked any number of times, particularly by men of means, why should anyone want to pay the expensive prices for a suit, shirt, or necktie? Whenever that question comes up, I am reminded of my early days at Bonwit Teller. Needless to say, as explained in earlier chapters, I wore the necessary clothes to get through the workday, whether as office boy in the president's office or, later, handling more advanced responsibilities in higher positions.

I was aware then, by watching young executives who worked in Bonwit Teller, particularly those who had a sense of style, what was required to fit in. They seemed to be properly dressed for whatever the occasion. Some, I became aware of, seemed to dress with more style than others. Tom Lee, the creative genius at Bonwit Teller who invited Salvador Dalí to do the Fifth Avenue windows, dressed impeccably and was also an early guide. *Esquire* magazine also recommended the proper attire for the young men returning from World War II. With that background, it seemed effortless to know what to wear in business or social occasions.

Luxury

As I became aware of the type of clothes that were required to keep pace with my advancing business career, I had to find a men's store that had what I needed at prices that I could afford. During the fifties and sixties, there were men's stores that had good-quality clothes at moderate prices in New York and other major cities. Wallachs was the store I chose. One reason was that the clothes looked right. The other reason was that they allowed you to pay one-third of the bill each month, which at that point, I could afford.

As I moved up to Bergdorf Goodman, I recognized the same desire for men to be well dressed that I experienced in my early days at Bonwit Teller. I also found a class of successful businessmen who selected their cars and sporting equipment the same way— they wanted the very best their money could buy. They wanted luxury as a lifestyle. There was another class of successful men who were comfortable with conservative clothes at more modest prices. Both, as we used to say, were "good citizens."

I decided that the businessman interested in luxury clothing was the customer of choice for building Bergdorf Goodman's men's business. Thus began my learning the men's luxury market, from London, Paris, and Milan.

My exposure to Hermès, Turnbull & Asser, Charvet, Brioni, Luciano Barbera, and Kiton, to name a very few of the very best, set a standard of luxury that I would follow for the rest of my career.

Quality

To learn more from the principals of all the luxury markets about their workmanship and availability for Bergdorf Goodman's Men's Store, I raised my personal objectives as well as the goals for the store. I visited nearly all the factories of every luxury collection to be carried at Bergdorf Goodman.

I won't go into too much detail about each of the men's fashion houses that I visited, other than to say, each and every one involved, without exception, were exceptional artisans who brought passion and a commitment to produce the very best. It was imperative to me to have the best workmen and women for design, tailoring by hand, finishing and dyeing, or whatever specialty was required to turn out a quality product for the apex of the luxury market.

I also learned in men's clothing that correct fit is paramount. In shirts, the correct collar style defines each luxury retailer. Men's neckwear, particularly Hermès, requires such rigid inspection that any number of ties would be discarded in order to achieve perfection. Producing fabrics at Luciano Barbera in Biella, Italy, left some Australian wool producers with the mistaken impression that their wool was cashmere, it was so finely woven.

Value

In life, every man has to decide what it is that represents who he is. Much of that can be projected by where he buys his clothes. In addition to Wallachs, mentioned earlier, there was also Weber & Heilbroner and others—now all gone. Brooks Brothers and J. Press are some of the great retailers that have taken their place. Paul Stuart, another wonderful retailer, would be considered upscale and updated classic.

A man wearing Paul Stewart, Brooks Brothers, or J. Press can be sure that he is wearing the proper clothing projecting his personality as upscale, somewhat conservative, knowing what he is wearing is clothing of good value.

A man wearing Hermès, Turnbull, or Charvet can feel comfortable that he is projecting the image, possibly conservative, but knowing that he is wearing the best quality his money can buy for style, value, fit, and longevity.

LESSON LEARNED

There are successful men whose background leaves them comfortable with conservative machine-made clothing that fits them reasonably well and projects the image they feel comfortable with. There also are men who appreciate the best restaurants, hotels, resorts, and clubs who feel comfortable wearing what they consider the best clothes. It is these men who carefully observe what others are wearing in order to determine their taste level. Both are right. It is the customer looking for the best quality with value built in that Bergdorf Goodman's Men's Store targeted as their customer with great success.

Self-Awareness in
Dressing for the Occasion

NDRÉ LEON TALLEY, an editor-at-large for *Vogue*, referring to Michelle Obama, wrote, "Everyone knows that people respond to the way you look when you run for office." His comment brought back memories of my very early age when I first became aware of how people dressed.

Looking at old family photographs of the twenties, the women in my mother's family (there were seven sisters) and their friends seemed to take great pains, time, and money (before the Great Depression) to dress properly and appropriately for every social occasion. Men did the same for business and recreation, also aware of the need or desire for creating the proper impression. Everyone seemed to know and care that people respond to the way you look, whether you happened to be running for office or not.

I particularly recall how the teachers of my public schools dressed with pride for their profession. My favorite teacher in the eighth grade, Mrs. Schreiner, always in style for that time, wore colorful print dresses. She was properly made up for her gray hair and her pink complexion. She left an impression, in my mind, of a real teacher. She instilled in us how to dress for the occasion and to show who and what you were. In her case, she represented a teaching professional.

It was clear as my family and my teachers set proper dressing standards, with my taste level I continued to appreciate people who "looked right" and had a "sense of awareness" of who they were. With the end of the Depression and during World War II, except for people serving in the military, those who could afford to be called well dressed continued to do so. I could also see with my early introduction into the business world, albeit at Bonwit Teller, a top fashion store, people from executives down who worked in retailing as well as the customers took pride in their appearance.

I observed the upheaval of the young population who first took to wearing jeans and T-shirts to object to the Vietnam War. Fortunately, they reverted to dressing like their elders when they entered the workforce.

It was the next generation that Senator Daniel Patrick Moynihan described as "defining deviance down," referring to the street language and fashion trends that started, in many cases, with inner-city minority youths. It was copied by many of the middle and upper class "to be cool."

Compounding this approach, many major professional offices adopted "Casual Fridays," which possibly started in Silicon Valley. Self-presentation deteriorated to such a degree that office staffs had to gradually work their way back to looking acceptable to the degree that professionals and their clients appreciated. One of the jokes about "dressing down" of that time was "dressing down is cheaper than dressing up." The response: "You look like you can't afford anything better."

It would seem that today, many young men and women dress for convenience and comfort, not for appearance. In the process they miss the opportunity of presenting themselves at their very best.

While growing up, observations of my family and later executives in my early retail fashion career formed my opinions about self-awareness in dressing. Watching dressing standards deteriorate particularly in the younger generation bothered me.

As I visited different universities around the country, I was struck by the photos on display in the hallways showing students in the thirties, forties, and fifties. These students conforming with their peers dressed as young ladies and gentlemen, compared to those students today, who looked as though they have no concern what they look like. They are concerned that dressing up and presenting themselves differently than their classmates would make them stand out—something to be avoided.

In 1975, when I became the CEO of Bergdorf Goodman, I felt, among many of my ambitions for the store, one was to make people more conscious of the best taste level possible. To help bring back, as it were, higher standards of dressing for the entire world to see and to desire.

The immediate strategy called for the updating and the transformation from the old Bergdorf Goodman to the new. The long-term strategy with an eye toward the not-too-distant future was to build a store for the very many emerging new wealthy and fashion-conscious women in the United States and abroad.

Fortunately, my ambition was made possible by the recent development and tremendous influx and acceptance of the French, Italian, and American fashion designers. The advent of the high-profile fashion designers inspired women who initially were hesitant to buy but possessed self-awareness to finally feel more confident projecting their desired image. A woman would feel confident saying, "I am wearing Chanel,

Armani, or Oscar (or the designer's lower-priced collections), and I am carrying an identifiable designer handbag (or a copy)."

Another ambition and determination of mine was that any customer shopping at Bergdorf Goodman and later the Men's Store would have available to them not only the finest merchandise in the world but professional salespeople. These professionals would assure their customers how to project the image they desired and to feel comfortable in the process.

To accomplish all my lofty ambitions, short- and long-term strategies were imperative. However, it was the talented and devoted personnel whose uppermost thoughts and service were focused upon the ideal that "The customer always comes first" who helped make Bergdorf Goodman the great fashion store on Fifth Avenue.

LESSON LEARNED

Dressing is like packaging. An attractive package is always front and center. The unattractive package is usually moved to the rear of the shelf.

Telephone Manners or Not

HAVE YOU NOTICED that as dress codes eroded over the past few years, telephone manners have deteriorated as well? One of the tell-tale signs of rudeness is made by someone who does not respond after a reasonable length of time to a phone message awaiting a reply. This usually indicates how important or unimportant the recipient feels about the caller. This would rarely happen in a person-to-person meeting, which would be considered a snub. Bad form.

Another bad habit has developed. A secretary or a receptionist, when asking you, "Who is calling?" and you respond with your name, replies, "One moment, please," using your first name. When that occurs, I ask the receptionist or the secretary, "Do I know you?" The usual reply is a hesitant "Sorry," or some other weak excuse, as he or she likely has not been trained properly or doesn't know any better.

As progress moves far ahead, Alexander Graham Bell would never have dreamed of cell phones or the misuse of them when he made that first, famous phone call to Mr. Watson. There is no question cell phones are as necessary for communication as cars are to transportation. However, it is bad form, and in some cities, illegal, to blow the car horn, annoying other drivers, pedestrians, and neighborhoods. Again, using a cell phone in an area disturbing to others telegraphs a lack of manners, possibly reflecting a poor upbringing, and displaying indifference to the immediate surroundings.

No one wants to be thought of as having a poor upbringing. However, there are those who show that lack loud and clear (no pun intended) by displaying little or no consideration for the people within their hearing range.

Possibly not considered bad telephone manners, but just as irritating, is hearing the answering machine at the other end requiring the caller to "Press one, two, three," and so on to reach the designated party. It would seem that successful businesspeople of yore understood the importance of their customers by employing telephone operators making connections to people or departments in that business. Today, unfortunately, too many financial people wield their influence by cutting costs and salaries by having computer programs and computer-generated voices do the work. Thus, the disconnect to customers many times over. In the process, not only did the professional salespeople disappear but courteous telephone operators also became a vanished breed as well.

It is puzzling that successful businesses spend millions and millions of advertising dollars to develop favorable and identifiable images. They then throw much of that away frustrating and angering their customers by forcing them to run through an endless loop of pushing buttons to discourage them from speaking with a person and the company harboring the added "expense" that entails.

Customers who are valued assets should be greeted by a person at the other end who reflects the company's desired image.

LESSONS LEARNED

To greet customers by their (proper) name has many advantages.

In the past and today, most people in our society attempt to show considerations in social situations. However, there are those among us who unfortunately have not been taught at home or at school that certain social situations require good manners. The same applies to businesses that have forgotten the importance of the human touch.

Black Tuesday, Green Friday

THOSE OF US WHO are old enough to recall or have read about Black Tuesday, the Wall Street Crash of 1929, will recall that it was the disaster that started the Great Depression. Black. A fitting color for the many people who went into mourning as an untold number of jobs, fortunes, homes, and lives were lost in that unmitigated disaster.

Fast-forward to about 1966. Someone, possibly the press, surely not an experienced retailer, coined the phrase Black Friday. This is the Friday following Thanksgiving when the press keeps stating that retailers go into the black.

First, let me say, any retailer who has to wait for the Friday after Thanksgiving to start making a profit is in the wrong business. True, the Friday after Thanksgiving is one of the busiest shopping days of the year. Fine. So it should be called Green Friday for the color of money because money is what retailing is all about. That day should be celebrated as positively as possible. Not with "black," as in mourning or the difference between red for loss and black for profit.

If a retailer hasn't been profitable by Thanksgiving, no matter what that day is called, black would be appropriate for that business's demise.

Salesmanship: The Road to Profit

I
N ALL ENDEAVORS there are examples of excellence whether in sports, business, finance, teaching, acting, or you name it. When it comes to the top stars in salesmanship, two people, as I observed over many years, made salesmanship look to be a high art.

The first was Stanley Marcus, for many years the president and CEO of Neiman Marcus. One story of his legendary salesmanship may be a myth, but knowing Mr. Stanley, as he was called by one and all at Neiman Marcus, it is most likely true.

A lady approached Mr. Stanley when he was on the selling floor and said that she wanted to buy a necktie for her husband. The tie was selected and sold. Then Mr. Stanley said, "I think you should have the proper shirt that would go with the tie." Again, the shirt was selected, again sold. Not to stop there, "Let me show you a wonderful suit and a hat that I am sure your husband would enjoy wearing." All sold to a happy customer. This is a perfect example of what was called multiple selling.

It doesn't matter whether the potential sale is at a luxury retailer like Neiman Marcus or a volume retailer. Any salesman or saleswoman who deserves that title also has the responsibility to show the customer another item that he or she senses the customer could be interested in.

My second nomination to the Salesman Hall of Fame (if there were such a pantheon) would be Michael Afshar. Mr. Afshar, known by all of his customers as Michael, was one of the head salesmen at Bergdorf Goodman's Men's Store.

Early on, I became aware of Michael's ability to give customers the security that he had a complete understanding of their needs and their concerns for looking right. Whenever I walked by Michael's department, possibly at least twice a day (again, putting into practice MBWA), Michael would always introduce me to celebrities from Hollywood and sports, TV news anchors, heads of state, et cetera, et cetera. His customer list is too large to list here. However, I recall his customer book required two hands to hold. The book was a treasure trove.

LESSON LEARNED

The two tales of salesmanship told here are extreme examples of selling in luxury markets. However, the principle of "Give the customer what he or she wants" is the basis for all salespeople to understand and to strive for at all levels of retailing. Unfortunately, too many retailers today were not brought up knowing the productivity that professional salespeople contribute. This lack of understanding has caused untold millions of dollars never to be spent in their stores.

Trading Down Our Fifth Avenue

OCCASIONALLY I HAVE the opportunity to visit Bergdorf Goodman, the Sherry Netherland, and the Plaza Hotel, as well as the wonderful Apple store, which is located in what was formerly the General Motors building. I might add, before that, it was the Savoy Plaza Hotel. The Grand Army Plaza was once as elegant an area to be found anywhere in the world.

It is a shock and disheartening to now see the many food, handbag, and pashmina scarf peddlers covering the area to the degree that they do. On a recent Sunday afternoon, Bergdorf Goodman not only had peddlers on 58th Street but along its complete front of Fifth Avenue, from 57th to 58th Street. The former General Motors building had peddlers all along their Fifth Avenue frontage, as well as on both 58th and 57th Streets. It seemed that the only buildings not covered by this infestation of peddlers were Donald Trump's Trump Tower and Tiffany & Co. They wisely placed very large flower-filled tubs in front of their prominent locations, making it unavailable for food and merchandise peddlers to depreciate what they both stand for.

5th Avenue Merchants Want a Ban on Vendors

By FELICIA R. LEE

Officials of some of New York's most prestigious Fifth Avenue stores — Tiffany's, Saks Fifth Avenue and Bergdorf Goodman — told a legislative hearing yesterday that street peddlers had turned the avenue into a flea market of haggling, hustling and counterfeit goods.

The merchants said the problem was especially bad this Christmas, as peddlers compete with stores for bargain-hunting shoppers. They said the peddlers clog pedestrian traffic around their stores, litter and try to engage prospective shoppers in illegal card games.

"New York needs the image of a healthy, glamorous Fifth Avenue," said Ira Neimark, chairman of Bergdorf Goodman. He read state legislators a letter from a customer who had complained that the world-famous shopping district had become "a sleazy main drag."

The hearing by the New York State Senate Committee on Investigations, Taxation and Government Operations was about New York City street vendors. In particular, the committee solicited information about the impact of state-licensed peddlers who are disabled veterans. They are exempt from municipal regulations on peddling.

Open-Air Markets

In April, the Appellate Division of State Supreme Court in Manhattan upheld an 1894 state law that gives special consideration to peddlers who are disabled veterans. The court ruled that the state law took precedence over a 1979 city ordinance that outlawed street peddlers from 30th Street to 65th Street between Second and Ninth Ave-

World-famous shopping district or 'a sleazy main drag?'

New Yorkers and a shopping mecca for millions of customers."

Mr. Goodman, a Manhattan Republican, said that while the peddlers were a problem throughout the city it is a particular problem for the Fifth Avenue stores because of the area's reputation. He said an informal survey by the investigations committee staff showed 166 street vendors on Fifth Avenue between 49th and 59th Streets one Sunday, selling everything from balloons to fake Cartier watches.

Joseph Kaswan, a 72-year-old disabled World War II veteran who sought the ruling on disabled peddlers, said yesterday that they had been unfairly blamed. He said he had personally appealed to the peddlers not to sell counterfeit goods and to carry proper papers.

"I am very disturbed when I hear people equating the elegance of Fifth Avenue with the blood of the men shed defending this country." Mr. Kaswan said.

Senator Goodman said he hoped to amend the state law to restrict business times and places for the disabled vendors while taking into account their need for jobs. New York City Councilwoman Carol Greitzer, Democrat of Manhattan, has called for the State Legislature to amend the law so that all veterans are subject to regulations.

A street peddler selling counterfeit designer sweatshirts in front of Tiffany's. State legislators heard testimony yesterday from Fifth Avenue merchants that the peddlers are ruining the street's glamorous image.

Street vendors outside of Fifth Avenue stores.

All this reminded me of the efforts made a number of years ago by Donald Trump and the Fifth Avenue merchants to rid the area of peddlers in order to restore the grandeur that was once a reflection of the best of New York City. There were press conferences held by Donald Trump and the merchants, as well as lobbying efforts in Albany, to rectify a law that had run wild. Peddlers were locating themselves on Fifth Avenue from below 34th all the way up to 60th Streets, on both sides of Fifth Avenue.

Fortunately, the law then that allowed indiscriminate peddling was changed, and stated that peddling must be done at designated areas in order not to depreciate the Grand Army Plaza and the elegance and history that it stands for.

LESSONS LEARNED

Being a good businessman also means being a good citizen.

As high standards are required in a successful business, so are they required in the society that surrounds us. Catering to the lowest common denominator will eventually bring you there.

The Internet and Retailing

T HIS BOOK WOULD not be complete without discussing how the Internet is greatly changing and challenging retailing today and the impact the Internet will have on traditional retailing going into the future.

David Pogue, computer specialist for *The New York Times*, recently summed up my feelings in a recent radio interview:

> Television was supposed to kill radio. DVDs were supposed to kill going to the theater. None of that ever happened. They coexist. Things just splinter. They just add on. New technologies just sort of pile on. Everyone keeps saying, "Oh my gosh, printed books are dead." No, they're just the e-book readers who will just add on.

A number of years ago, the Sears Roebuck catalog, as well as the Spiegel catalog, was the shoppers' bible. Today high-grade catalogs such as Neiman Marcus's Christmas catalog and many others continue to draw many customers. There are also direct-mailing pieces today that are stuffed in mailboxes and many come with the daily newspapers.

However—slowly at first; now rapidly, in many cases—the Internet has increased to the point that more retail sales are made online than through direct mail, and this will continue to grow exponentially.

For the long foreseeable future, there will be less direct mail and major increases in Internet sales for retailers like Macy's, Bloomingdales, Nordstrom's, Neiman Marcus, Bergdorf Goodman, and Saks Fifth Avenue, just to name a very few.

The caveat to the above is that as long as customer service continues to deteriorate in many of the specialty and department stores, the success of their in-store businesses is in jeopardy.

The question is often asked, what will happen to the luxury retailers (and others) with the Internet growing at such a rapid rate? Will brick-and-mortar stores stay in business?

Stores such as Bergdorf Goodman, Neiman Marcus, and Hermès will, of course, continue to prosper for any number of reasons brought up throughout this book. But for the question of the survival of the brick-and-mortar stores in general, it is useful to note the miracle of the Apple stores. No matter where and when you go to visit an Apple store, it is busy. During the weekends, especially, it is mobbed.

All these Apple customers have and use computers. Sitting at home or in their office, they can order any Apple product any time they want online. However, these customers also enjoy the shopping experience of being in an environment surrounded with other customers, with a wide assortment of merchandise that they desire, and with many knowledgeable salespeople readily available and eager to assist them.

The fact that Internet shopping is available to customers 24 hours a day, seven days a week, with tremendous assortments, will accomplish, at the very least, two objectives. First, customers at every income level living in cities without a major retailer can, with great ease, purchase merchandise from these same retailers, as well as from retailers they never knew existed. Second, the lack of salespeople, knowledgeable or not, has discouraged many customers from enduring the frustrating experience of poor customer service within brick-and-mortar stores that lack the appeal and personal attention of the Apple stores.

One of the best examples of customer service on the Internet is the Gilt Groupe. Even though this company sells high-end fashion merchandise at deep discounts, its customer service policy mirrors what traditional retailers understood in the past—exactly what was so necessary to build customer loyalty and sales.

Surely, the Internet through retail's continuous evolution will eliminate the need for fringe retailers. They will have served their purpose, as family-owned regional department stores served theirs, and eventually disappear from the retail scene.

LESSON LEARNED

Giving the customer what he or she wants has never gone out of style. From the peddlers of old to the newest methods of distribution, customers will always buy from whomever has the desired merchandise and from whomever has the ability to serve them efficiently and easily.

"From Where I Sit"

SAM FEINBERG WAS THE SENIOR WRITER for *Women's Wear Daily* in the mid-twentieth century. A wise and as fair a reporter as there ever was. His columns, "From Where I Sit," in August and October 1975, regarding the change of ownership of the retail industry and the management changes they brought about, are worth a book in themselves.

In his August column, he tells of the passing of the descendents of retail dynasties—the Lazurus Brothers of Federated Department Stores, Adam Gimbel of the Gimbel/Saks chain, Morton May of May Department Stores, and Richard Rich of Rich's. He goes on to say that Stanley Marcus and Andrew Goodman sold their stores to Carter Hawley Hale and remained involved.

The October column describes the executives in their forties and fifties who took over as heads of these stores. It reads like a blue book of retailing.

These columns represent the tectonic shift that took place in retailing in a very short period of time.

From Where I Sit

August 26, 1975

By Sam Feinberg

Family lines have continued in command of retail companies longer than in business in general. The reason is that the world of store chains is closer to its beginnings as big business than are the industrial giants. After all, professional management in retailing dates back only to 1906 when Sears, Roebuck pioneered the sale of public securities.

A number of descendants of founders of retail dynasties have died in the past decade. Among them are three Lazarus brothers of Federated Department Stores—Fred Jr., Jeffrey Sr. and Robert Sr; Bernard F. and Adam L. Gimbel of the Gimbels-Saks chains; Morgan J. May of May Department Stores, and Richard H. Rich, Rich's.

The retirement of Bruce A. Gimbel, 62, as chairman of Gimbel Bros, at the end of this month marks the departure of the fourth generation of Gimbels (the fifth generation, represented by Robert, Bruce's son, left the firm several years ago in favor of Wall Street).

Ralph Lazarus, Fred's son, is due to relinquish his Federated chairmanship within the next few years, after which only a handful of Lazari of the fourth and fifth generations will continue to occupy corporate or divisional posts. John Ralph Lazarus, one of Ralph's three sons, is an assistant buyer at the Filene's division. Richard Rich's son Michael P. is a senior vice-president at the family-founded regional chain. Fifth-generation Kenneth H. Straus is a senior vice-president at R. H. Macy & Co.

Of course, professional management—the power of performance over pull—need not be confined to outsiders. It can be—and has been—exercised by family members. However, in the past, poorly prepared men, bolstered by sizable family stockholdings, have often been perpetuated along with those who fill high-echelon positions strictly on merit. Increasingly, for competitive reasons, the family has had to seek an orderly transition at the helm regardless of ancestry.

Among the steadily declining number of family members remaining as chairmen of department store chains are G. Stockton Strawbridge, Strawbridge & Clothier; William B. Thalhimer Jr., Thalhimer Bros.; Kenneth M. Dayton, Dayton-Hudson; Joseph L. Hudson Jr., Dayton-Hudson's J. L. Hudson division; and George M. Ivey. Bernard and Robert T. Sakowitz are, respectively, chairman and president of Sakowitz. Stanley Marcus is chairman of Neiman-Marcus's executive committee, while his son Richard C. is president.

Since Gimbel Bros. was taken over two years ago by Brown & Williamson Tobacco Co., American subsidiary of London-based British-American Tobacco Co., a number of executive and operating changes have been effected. Within the past three months, Paul A. Salomone has left as president of Gimbels New York and Richard G. Shapiro has resigned as president of Gimbel Bros. Bruce A. Gimbel has retired as chairman of the national Gimbel chain and Martin S. Kramer has succeeded him. Kramer comes from Allied Stores but was at one time with Gimbels' Pittsburgh store. In a restructuring of Gimbels and Saks, the operations of the two chains have been separated and Allan R. Johnson, Saks' chairman, now reports directly to Louisville-based Brown & Williamson Industries where his superiors are Joseph E. Edens, president and chief executive officer, and Edward A. Scully, executive vice-president.

Last month, Robert Sakowitz moved up from vice-president of Sakowitz, the Hudon-based, privately-owned specialty store chain, to president, and his father Bernard assumed the new post of chairman as well as chief executive. Bernard says this should assure family ownership for at least another generation. He believes "It's a tragedy when a guy like Stanley Marcus, a guy like Grover Magnin sells a company. As stores get absorbed by big groups, they say they'll not change, but there's got to be a change. You're responsible to a whole new group. The only people I have to please are Ann (his wife), myself, Bob and my daughter (Lynn Wyatt)."

The elder Sakowitz is referring to mergers of Neiman-Marcus, and Bergdorf Goodman into Carter Hawley Hale within the past half dozen years. In the case of Grover Magnin, Sakowitz's long memory takes him back to Bullock's purchase of I. Magnin & Co. in 1944 and the merger of Bullock's-Magnin in 1964 into Federated which later separated that division into two subsidiaries.

Asked for comment on Sakowitz's statement, Stanley Marcus responds: "I don't want to get involved in any controversy. This is a free country." Having said which, he adds: "Under the ownership of 'C double H,' we do better planning than before and have improved our net profit substantially. No, I won't tell you what our net is and I have no idea what Sakowitz' is. If I were doing it over again, I would have done it five years earlier. I'm extremely pleased with our new team" (the two Dicks—president Richard Marcus and chairman Richard P. Hauser, who was recruited from Bloomingdale's last January).

The elder Marcus was reached in his new Dallas office near Neiman's downtown store. He reports that, as executive vice-president of CHH, he usually spends four or five hours a day three days a week at the store and one or two days a month at Bergdorf's and Holt Renfrew, the parent company's Canadian specialty store chain.

The 70-year-old Marcus is "in fine health" and plans to retain his Neiman and CHH posts for the foreseeable future. In addition to his corporate duties, he finds time to help publicize his book, "Minding the Store," through personal appearances. The book has done "very well" in this country and in England and will be published in Japan next year.

Andrew Goodman decided to sell Bergdorf's following the resignation as vice-president of his son Edwin to work, first, for the Bedford-Stuyvesant Development and Service Corp, and, then, for WBAI, a listener-supported, New Left radio station, of which he is general manager. Two sons-in-law of Andrew also opted for non-retail careers after occupying Bergdorf posts for a number of years.

Earlier this year, Andrew Goodman, 68, was succeeded as president and chief executive officer by Ira Neimark, previously executive vice-president at B. Altman. Goodman now serves as chairman. Neal J. Fox was transferred from Neiman's where he was senior vice-president and general merchandise manager to Bergdorf's as executive vice-president and genm. Leonard J. Hankin continues as executive vice-president for store management.

From Where I Sit

October 8, 1975
By Samuel Feinberg

At least 20 men in their 40s or younger have risen to chairman or president of leading retail companies this year—more than those in any other age range. This trend has been intensifying over the past 10 to 15 years since family and other long-entrenched management has given way to younger people with educational and store backgrounds entitling them to high professional status.

The most recent examples of the call for relative youth in the control booth are Joseph E. Brooks, 47; chairman, Lord & Taylor; Franklin Simon, 49, president, Filene's; Kai Frost, 44, president, Gimbels-Philadelphia, and

Robert B. Cockayne, 37, president, May Cohens.

At the same time, men in their 50s and over are not being ignored, as witness Martin S. Kramer and Elliot Stone, each 54, respectively chairman and president, Gimbel Bros., and Norman V. Wechsler, 63, president, l. Magnin & Co.

Among other top-job changes in the 40-to-50-year age bracket this year:

Melvin Jacobs, 49, chairman, Burdine's; Alan B. Gilman, 44, president, Abraham & Straus; John W. Christian Jr., 49, president, B. Altman & Co.; Richard R. Pivirotto, 45, and William P. Arnold, 50, respectively chairman and president, Associated Dry Goods Corp.; David C. Farrell, 42, president, May Department Stores; Donald J. Stone, 45, chairman, Foley's; Denny Arvanites, 44, chairman, May Co., Cleveland; Joseph S. Davis, 45, president, G. Fox & Co.; Richard P. Hauser, 40, chairman, Neiman-Marcus; Harvey Sanford, 49, president, Titche's; C. Hal Silver, 50, president, Kaul-

mann's; Charles Heller, 47, president, Stewart's, Baltimore; John C. Seiler, about 40, president, Stewart's, Louisville; Carrick A. Hill, 42, president, Denver Dry Goods Co., and John Schumacher, 43, group president, Genesco's women's specialty stores.

Still others in their 40s who have made it to the top command; Robert J. Suslow, president, Famous-Barr; Sanford J. Zimmerman, chairman, A&S; Angelo Arena, president, The Emporium, and M. Ronald Ruskin, president, May-D&F.

More executives in the 40-to-50 magic circle: Howard Goldfeder, chairman, Bullock's; Marvin S. Traub, president, Bloomingdale's; Merwin F. Kaminstein, president, Donaldson's; David R. Waters, president, Garfinckel, Brooks Bros., Miller & Rhoads; Joel Goldberg, president, Rich's; Arnold Aronson, president, Bullock's; Jack L. Richardson, chairman, Capwell's; Arthur L. Crowe, president, Weinstock's, and Richard L. Battram and James H. Coe, respectively president and chairman, Mejer & Frank.

Among other of this year's appointees in their 50s are Ira Neimark, 52, president, Bergdorf Goodman and Stanley Abelson, 52, president, Lit Bros.

Among presidents in their 30s are Howard P. Goldberg, 36, Ohrbach's; Richard C. Marcus, 37, Neiman-Marcus, and Macdonald Clark, 36, Robinson's of Florida.

Joe Brooks' philosophy of leadership should be of interest to anyone who holds or aspires to upper-echelon management. At Filene's, as in his previous high posts at Rike's and Burdine's, he expressed his views in a memo to buyers and other executives entitled "Our Responsibility in the Development of People." His statement in part:

"Qualities to be cultivated in development—Motivation as the reason and the purpose for action. Inspiration in bringing others to greater performance; expecting and extracting the highest standards. Supervision of people as individuals, being demanding but fair for the individual and for the business. Tolerance in having respect for others, their opinions, methods and mannerisms. Flexibility in being willing to listen and carefully balancing the desires of learning and teaching at the same time. Objectivity in people as well as situations, rationally appraising performances. Courage in being willing to stand up for one's beliefs despite opposition. Enthusiasm in supporting decisions made with which you are not in agreement but demanded because of membership on management's team. Honesty and integrity in your dealings with people; say before them what you would say behind them."

Brooks added his conviction on the difference between being a boss or a leader: "A boss drives, a leader coaches. A boss inspires fear, a leader inspires enthusiasm. A boss says 'I', a leader says 'we'. A boss fixes the blame, a leader fixes mistakes. A boss knows how, a leader shows how. A boss makes the job a drudgery, a leader makes it a game. A boss depends on authority, a leader depends on good will.

In a special report, "Young Top Management," *Businessweek* tells "how dedicated under-40 executives are making it big." Among those interviewed were John H. Bryan Jr., 38, president, Consolidated Foods Corp.; Wilfred J. Corrigan, 37, President, Fairchild Camera & Instrument Corp.; Richard S. Ravenscroft, 36, president, Philadelphia National Bank, and Richard L. Kattel, 39, chairman, Atlanta's Citizens & Southern National Bank.

Kattel is quoted: "You have to surround yourself with people who are pros themselves in given areas and seek out their knowledge. What I have really done is surround myself with entrepreneurs who are professionals in their own right."

Stressing the need for individual drive, the article finds: "That kind of drive is just what many experienced managers are looking for when they fill the top spots in their own organizations. The trend toward youth in the executive suite may be just beginning. Fifteen years ago, the median age of executives attending advanced management programs at the University of Southern California was 48. Today, the median age is 43 and the 30-year-old is becoming a frequent participant."

Some companies are still reported to shy away from youthful managers in top slots. Many recruiters claim that older executives are also coming in their own, even as candidates for jobs in other companies.

Both articles reprinted with permission from Women's Wear Daily.

LESSON LEARNED

Whenever your field of endeavor is crowded with equally qualified executives, it is important to have at least one proven talent that stands out from all the rest. The other requirement is to have a network of executives who are in a position to make known that special talent to potential employers.

Lessons Learned Fast-Forward

TWO EXCELLENT EXAMPLES of today's very successful retailers who came up through the ranks are Karen Katz, CEO of The Neiman Marcus Group, and Jim Gold, president of Specialty Retail, The Neiman Marcus Group. Both have achieved remarkable results at Neiman Marcus and Bergdorf Goodman by staying with quality and service in the tradition of what these stores stand for.

Jim Gold, president of Specialty Retail, The Neiman Marcus Group. (Photo by Steve Eichner courtesy of Women's Wear Daily.*)*

Karen Katz, Executive Vice President of Neiman Marcus, poses in the front row at the Oscar de la Renta Spring 2007 fashion show during Olympus Fashion Week in the Tent in Bryant Park September 11, 2006 in New York City. (Photo by Peter Kramer/Getty Images.)

5

LESSONS LEARNED
from MY CAREER

LESSONS FOR
FUTURE SUCCESS

Looking Back, Looking Forward

I STARTED TO WRITE *The Rise of Fashion and Lessons Learned at Bergdorf Goodman* just before the recent economic crises. I realized as I was writing about past retail history, this economic disaster was happening to many retailers right before my eyes. Taking the liberty of quoting George Santayana, "Those who cannot remember the past are condemned to repeat it."

To my dismay, many retailers fell into the trap of reducing, and in some cases eliminating, their sales force. They may have reduced their expenses, but in the process, their sales suffered greatly. Compounding this strategy, poorly managed inventories caused further financial havoc. Many customers benefiting from these extravagant markdowns that were taken on new merchandise were left wondering, when will the next sale be? Or asking a salesperson, "When will this be marked down?"

Now that the recession is slowly passing, retailers are comparing their sales figures to last year, instead of the year before the recession, a more accurate comparison. I felt it my responsibility since I was on the scene to explain what happened to many retailers who emerged successfully from the Great Depression and the growth of the luxury fashion business since that time.

Cover of Esquire Trade Talk, *November 1991, featuring (from left) Geoffrey Beene, Bill Blass, Ira Neimark, and Calvin Klein. (Photo courtesy of Ira Neimark.)*

Adding to the excitement of the growth of the luxury fashion business were the fashion designers, retailers, and, of course, the movers and shakers of recent fashion history. To all of them, I wish continued success and a parting reminder: Never forget that looking back is as important as looking forward. With this in mind, I offer a compilation below of Lessons Learned, culled into a list from my first book, *Crossing Fifth Avenue to Bergdorf Goodman.*

Lessons Learned at Bergdorf Goodman

FROM THE VERY FIRST DAY of my business career, I became aware that there were certain steps necessary to become noticed by key executives, customers, and fellow employees.

Executives, I noticed, were particularly aware and always looking for bright young people. Customers were looking to be treated with common courtesy, respect, and recognition. Fellow employees, when not feeling threatened, could go a long way to helping achieve immediate objectives.

With this in mind, this list of Lessons Learned was developed over many successful business years, hopefully to be passed on to younger generations who will follow:

1. To get the job, make sure you fit the uniform or whatever else is required to get your foot in the door.

2. Whenever the situation requires innovation, innovate.

3. People like to be greeted with eye contact.

4. Greeting customers by their name has many advantages.

5. It is important that the environment and the atmosphere of the company suit your personality in order to maximize your ability.

6. Selecting an ideal role model at an early age is important and requires mature judgment. Those who do so go on to success; those who do not have a much more difficult row to hoe.

7. When required to talk to the press, be as positive as possible about whatever the subject.

8. When a photographer is present, face the camera.

9. Satisfying customers is and has always been the key to business success, whether greeting customers or being able to fulfill their needs for whatever merchandise or service that is being sold.

10. It is sometimes wise to accept a reduction in salary or position if it leads to a greater opportunity.

11. Always bet with other people's money.

12. It is not so much what you know but how you execute what you know.

13. Opportunity is always all around you. Another key to success is to be able to identify and develop the opportunity.

14. In planning a career, aim as high as you can. You may not hit the target at the top, but coming close is better than not aiming at all.

15. Never forget salespeople, designers, and manufacturers. If you have them on your side, you will be a successful merchant.

16. To be able to put yourself in the mind of the customer as to what it is he or she thinks is his or her requirement is half the battle. The other half is to meet that requirement.

17. If you are going to be a merchant, you have to gamble on your judgment. If your judgment is poor, you will be too.

18. The salespeople always know what merchandise is easiest to sell. They can tell a best seller before the buyers. They can, in most cases, tell what isn't going to be easy to sell, and can also tell at what price it should and will sell for.

19. Repeat. If you have the salespeople on your side, you will succeed; if the salespeople are not, you will increase your chances of failure.

20. Drink if you will, but not on other people's money.

21. If you want to create a good impression, always let your management know that you are interested in and dedicated to your job.

22. If you don't know how or why to make a merchandising procedure successful, keep your eyes and ears open until you find the person who has the answer.

23. It is most important to know the background and history of the company where you hope to build your career. Understanding and appreciating the culture and the background of the successful executives you will be working with is imperative to "fitting in."

24. The starting salary for a new job should be of secondary importance. It is the opportunity that the job offers for the future that is important.

25. The major reason for high markdowns and lower profit in many retail enterprises is the lack of professional planning practices.

26. It is most important whenever possible to have a fairy godmother or a godfather (sometimes called a rabbi) to guide you through the minefields of the business world and keep you pointed in the right direction to reach your goals.

27. In many cases when a successful retailer, defined as a strong sales and profit growth company with a growing customer base, is purchased, the new owner is often too hasty in wanting the store to change to his or her concept. In more cases than not, this is the recipe for failure.

28. Slow-moving and old inventory will strangle any business no matter how many management changes are made.

29. Again, it is what you know as well as who you know that get results. It never hurts and is very helpful to know people in high places.

30. A ready-to-wear inventory is only as good as its newest merchandise.

31. Never, never appoint a person to be a buyer unless he or she has been a proven success first as an assistant buyer. A rare exception may be made if the buying candidate is very bright and has a smart merchandise manager to give direction and supervision.

32. There is always a magic price. The trick is to be realistic and determine at what price customers will really be excited. Too many times buyers will decide at what price they would like a sale to be a success, not at what price the customer will find exciting.

33. Adjusting to a new position, examine carefully what the successes were as well as the failures of your predecessor before embarking on a different strategy.

34. The more you can think and shop like your customer, not like a buyer, the more successful you will be.

35. Deciding when to leave one position for another requires a great deal of thought for your career objectives. Additional advice from experienced executives should be part of the final decision.

36. A good merchant should have an organized sense of urgency. Not taking the immediate steps necessary to move slow-moving, unwanted merchandise in order to make room for new desirable merchandise has led to the demise of more retailers than I dare to count.

37. Retailing does not exist in a vacuum. Any and all the information you need to be a successful merchant is out there if you have the sense to know what you should be looking for and where to look for it.

38. Whenever possible, associate with successful business executives. Smart executives are always looking for talented people. It is better to be known than to be a face in the crowd.

39. Convincing employees to use a different method from what they are used to is always a difficult task. Motivating them to change requires convincing them that the change will benefit them greatly. If they can't be motivated, they must be directed. If they can't be directed, they should be removed.

40. The ability for a buyer to correctly find and negotiate for the "magic price" has always been the successful formula for moving sale merchandise. Filene's Basement understood this better than many regular retailers ever did.

41. Don't wait for desirable merchandise or opportunity to come to you. You must go after both.

42. In retailing there are many important positions, but none as important as a talented buyer. Executives who can identify, develop, and encourage talent are critical to a retailer's success.

43. If a retailer has made an investment and commitment to be in business, the customer has a right to expect the retailer will also fulfill its responsibility of carrying as complete an assortment of whatever it is the store stands for.

44. Watch every trend in retail distribution. There are new concepts being developed every day—some successful, some not. Analyze the successful trends to see if any part can be used to your advantage.

45. Whenever a job opportunity is offered, it is most desirable, if possible, to clear the decision with the former as well as the future employer. This will not be possible in all cases, but the effort should be made, if for no other reason than the executives will likely see each other over the years at social and business events.

46. A new position offers new opportunities. It is important to integrate slowly in order for people to feel they know you and what you stand for. Acceptance cannot be achieved overnight. As difficult as it may be, patience will always win out.

47. Whenever a new executive joins a company, the other executives will circle like sharks attempting to find his or her weak spots. Tact and superior knowledge will win out.

48. If for any reason you are going to take the risk of contradicting your boss, be sure that whatever it is you do is going to be a success.

49. When asked for ideas or suggestions from one of the highest executives in the company, it is important to keep the key executives in the loop. They will not like being upstaged but will appreciate that they were not kept in the dark. It also gives them the opportunity to be able to comment negatively or positively instead of just sitting there with egg on their face.

50. If you are put in the position of competing with your peers publicly, develop a business strategy to make a good showing.

51. Never present the person that you are hoping to replace with an analysis showing how wrong his or her strategy is compared to other leaders in the business.

52. No matter how undesirable a request from management may be, consider the long-range implications. As in many situations in life, you must consider if the gamble is worth taking. Seeking good advice from people with successful experience will help you arrive at the correct decision.

53. It is important to become familiar with the background and culture of the company you become associated with. The owners and principals appreciate, and require, that interest be shown by executives as a matter of pride and understanding of the business principles used by the company.

54. If management wants you to take on an unpleasant assignment, as difficult a decision as it may be, do it with the understanding that the risk may exceed the reward in the long run.

55. No matter what type of business you are involved with, decide who you want to be and what customer you want to appeal to.

56. Motivating an organization when the past has been bleak requires enthusiasm and courage. Make everyone in the organization know what the plan is in broad detail. Outline to the managers of the business the overall plan in greater detail. And be "consistently consistent."

57. It is most important to articulate what your standards are, and to be sure that the standards are monitored frequently and consistently so that there is no question whether employees completely understand what is required.

58. Whenever a question arises, say, regarding a customer service, no one should have to go to the company manual for an answer. Everyone should say, what would management expect me to do in this situation? And act accordingly. It will work many more times than not.

59. In a retail store and many other types of businesses, maintaining basic stock books, now computer programmed, is a given. Just like brushing your teeth at least twice a day. No imagination is required, but it has to be done. When you turn on the light switch, you expect the light to go on; when a customer asks for a basic item or size he or she desires, the customer expects it to be in stock. The alternative is not only a lost sale but also the potential loss of the customer.

60. The taking of markdowns can be developed into a profitable way to do business if the markdown is taken early enough, allowing money from the sale of the reduced merchandise to be reinvested in new merchandise. Experience shows most buyers and very few division buyers know or care to do this, hence, lost business, lower gross margins, and eventually red ink on the bottom line.

61. Nothing is forever, good times or bad. Be aware and always be prepared for the possibility of change, as you would be for any natural disaster.

62. In all difficult situations, there are things to learn and good people to meet.

63. No matter how professional and successful a company might be, particularly in a takeover, if the new business culture is different enough to make you feel ineffective and untrue to your potential, consider how to move on. Otherwise in the long run there will be unhappiness and frustration on both sides, which is a double negative not worth enduring.

64. Whenever there is a change in ownership in any business, the new owner will invariably have in mind management changes. Executives at different ages have different challenges.

65. The young executive is usually protected by lack of seniority and can ride out and may benefit from the change.

66. The senior executive is usually most at risk. Be prepared for a change in your position, either for someone to replace you or an executive above you who will want the change.

67. In the case of the senior executive, keep your options open by always being aware of and discreet about opportunities that are available in other companies.

68. Keep your nose to the grindstone. Working hard and long to achieve your objectives is bound to be recognized by your superiors and your colleagues—as well as your competition.

69. Try not to show your frustration when management changes take place that you have no control over. Do your job to the best of your ability, and keep your eyes open for opportunities at another company that will appreciate your talents.

70. Always look for smart people. The way to tell if they are smart is to see how sincere they are in describing their personal ambitions. If their ambitions are similar to yours, you will be able to tell how sincere they are by your understanding and relating to their goals and objectives.

71. It is always important to make a good first impression with your peers and superiors. In merchandising, to demonstrate that you know how to present and to move fashion merchandise is a good way to start.

72. Finding and being able to identify talented merchants is critical to success. Therefore, it becomes necessary for potential talent to demonstrate their merchandising ability. This can best be done by observing how aware the merchant is to current trends, not too attached to what was, but more interested in what will be.

73. If you can help it, never deal with amateurs, or people who don't know how to maximize their responsibility. Find a professional; it makes life easier and more profitable for everyone.

74. Newspapers, like all businesses, have knowledgeable and ambitious people. If you help them, they will help you. Helping does not mean leaking confidential information. This may be considered a favor, but it doesn't garner respect.

75. Unless the story is of major importance, give the story to the newspaper that will reach your audience. The caveat here is to be sure you explain to the newspaper that didn't get the desired story first that it will be made up for the next time.

76. Releasing the same story to all the press at one time may be safe, beneficial, and diplomatic, but again, newspapers, like all businesses, want to be first. You must select the medium that best serves your market.

77. As in all businesses, it is important to know and to be familiar with the major players. Being able to discuss and have entrée to their expertise will always broaden your knowledge.

78. Travel will always broaden your experiences. It is important to always explore every opportunity. The best opportunities may come from the most unexpected places.

79. Remember, one transaction each year that will cover your annual salary will be rewarded and appreciated by everyone involved in your future.

80. Always look for the opportunity to be exposed to the thinking of smart women in the retail world. This can be a major benefit to the understanding of the woman customer.

81. Whenever a resource selects your store (no matter how large or small) for the introduction of a new product, the executive concerned must notify the senior executive in order for the product to be judged by more than one person.

82. Whenever the opportunity presents to meet the leaders of the industry that you are involved with, do so.

83. As uplifting a feeling as it is to join a company that you have long admired as the CEO or any other major management position, it is most important that the previous management of that company and you have a clear understanding of the specific and clearly written job responsibilities of all the executives involved.

84. As difficult as it is to leave a company that you feel has been helpful in your career, particularly in being close to the senior executives, it is most important to leave on the best of terms possible. Your paths will undoubtedly cross many times.

85. Whenever you take on a new responsibility, it is imperative to study the previous administration's strategies, as well as its strengths and weaknesses. The same study applies to your competition.

86. Business executives who are insulated and live in a vacuum tend not to see growth opportunities. It is important to measure your performance against your peers. One of the first measurements is productivity, that is, sales per square foot. The second is gross profit per square foot. The comparisons are easily available if you look for them. The next important step is to act on the information.

87. Business principles and standards must be set and maintained. Principles as to what you stand for should never be compromised, and standards should never be lowered.

88. When a company is taking over an underperforming business, it is important to analyze the strengths as well as the weaknesses of the business. The strengths should be developed and the weaknesses eliminated. This applies to merchandise as well as people.

89. It is important that all levels of personnel be made aware of what the goals and ambitions for the business are. They, in turn, in carrying out their responsibilities must reflect the chief executive's vision for the company.

90. In considering opportunities of any nature, business ethics should be at the top of the list of not only retailers but all businesspeople. Fine reputations can be destroyed by lapses in good and honest judgment.

91. In attempting to imbue a store with personality, to make it clear what it stands for, and to determine who your customer is, you need exquisite and defining judgment. A top-flight fashion director can best do the balancing to keep the older customer and attract the younger customer. Over the years I have noticed some retailers asked their spouses for advice. Not recommended.

92. Asking professionals, as well as customers, their opinion regarding your efforts will give you some candid thoughts you may not have been aware of.

93. A good idea, whether old or new, is a good idea. Going back to the French couture to jump-start Bergdorf Goodman's fashion image worked beyond our fondest dreams. Fashion-conscious customers are always interested when the fashion press recognizes exciting ideas.

94. "Front-page news is front-page fashion" applies appropriately to the reintroduction of the French couture to Bergdorf Goodman.

95. Whatever ingredients are required to complete the successful product mix of a company, identifying the right ingredient is first, and determination and tenacity to procure the merchandise is next.

96. When building a business, you have to know both who your present customer is and who you want your new customer to be. After that, the objective is deciding what type of merchandise or service will satisfy them both.

97. When you are trying to revitalize a business, there is almost always something—a trend, product line, or expert—that has enough recognition in your industry to redefine your company's meaning in the eyes of customers. As soon as you discover this critical element, it is imperative that you pull out all the stops to align your company with this new direction.

98. To be successful in the fashion business, as in other businesses, there are three basic elements required for success: (1) Is the concept correct for the business? As a corollary, what does the business stand for? (2) Is the financing appropriate? (3) Is the organization professional? All three are required; otherwise, the business will collapse like a house of cards.

99. Successful business relationships are best developed when both parties understand and agree to their mutual objectives. Writing down these objectives as in any contract will help to eliminate any misunderstanding.

100. If you believe what you are doing is right, stick to your guns. Successful results will overcome nearly all adversity.

101. Whenever taking on a responsibility that requires the previous executive to be involved, a clear understanding between both parties as to each executive's responsibilities is imperative. It must be understood that in most cases previous executives will be reluctant to turn over responsibilities in areas where they feel they have a superior background.

102. It is important to be successful in the initial changes in order to convince everyone involved that you are on the right track. The more people telling the previous management that they made the right decision to bring you on board, the easier the transition.

103. Constant communication with your market principals and your own executives minimizes any signals or direction confusion that may occur from time to time.

104. When the chief executive asks you to lunch, and you have a previous appointment for an important lunch, invite the executive along.

105. A store or restaurant, like a person, must have a personality. The personality must be geared to the customer you are trying to attract. Consistency, recognition, and/or good merchandise or food are necessary but are not the only key elements.

106. Some executives tend to view a business from the expense reduction opportunities. Merchants view a business from its growth opportunities. Both are right. However, it becomes a matter of not putting the cart before the horse. A merchant's responsibility is to build sales profitably. Financial people should manage expenses in order to grow the profit of the business. But without sales growth, there will be no additional expenses to manage.

107. When a strategic decision is made by a company, it is most important that all concerned—executives, employees, suppliers, customers, and the press—be given the positive reasons for the decision; otherwise, negative thinking can snowball. Sometimes selling the positive is more like pushing water uphill. But the positive must prevail.

108. Being the last man standing confirmed my philosophy that tenacity, hard work, and a lot of good luck is a combination tough to beat.

109. "Build a better mousetrap" or "build a great baseball team and they will come" are not empty phrases. If the management of the business stresses service and uniqueness, as well as complete and broad assortments of whatever is to be sold, it will be a success.

110. Retailing requires showmanship. No matter what type of store, customers and the press relate to drama and presentation. Fashion-interested customers do not need "new clothes," but they do need clothes that bring about an exciting feeling and conversation.

111. The press has always been and will always be helpful to those merchants who show creative merchandising and business ability. On the other hand, the press can do much harm to a retailer who appears not to be holding on to and not building its share of the market.

112. When you are determining a marketing strategy, it is imperative to know who your customer was, is, and will be. Equally as important is to know what type of environment this customer feels comfortable in. (This applies to fashion stores as well as department and discount stores.) Who the future customer will be is most important, since the future is now.

113. The new "European" second floor, realizing a rapid growth of sales and profit, was a high-profile reason that Carter Hawley Hale could claim that the capital budget invested in Bergdorf Goodman on Fifth Avenue was possibly one of the best retail investments ever made.

114. Fashion, like any other business, has its stars. It is important to be able to identify the present leaders, but it is even more important to find the new talent before the competition does.

115. There is a tremendous competitive advantage if you can arrange to have the best merchandise lines exclusive to your store or business. Today the designers' distribution strategy makes this approach almost impossible. However, it can still be done if you structure exclusive arrangements that will benefit the designer as well.

116. Nothing is forever; marketing is always in a state of change. Customer acceptance and loyalty is only maintained when the retailer or designer create the merchandise, the image, and the environment that stimulates the customer in order to satisfy his or her desires.

117. Short-range planning will help to keep you in business a short time. Long-range planning will keep you there much longer.

118. The store's fashion directors know before the buyers who are or will be the new successes. It is the function of the buyer to make the designer selected by the fashion office a merchandising success. It is not the function of the fashion office to enhance the prestige of a buyer's selection for a "safe designer's collection."

119. Good press will speed a talented designer on to success. Bad press will speed a mediocre designer on to his or her demise.

120. In retailing as in other businesses, productivity is the key to success. High sales and gross margin productivity will bring a good merchant great success. Low productivity will always eventually bring failure.

121. In the fashion business, it is just as important to have the best talent available for fashion guidance, as it is for financial, operational, and merchandising guidance.

122. It is also important to have the merchandise division recognize that the head of the company often makes the key decisions for supporting the fashion executives. It is not for the people in merchandising divisions to decide that they don't require guidance and they can do just as well on their own. Those who feel they can do so should be let go to do just that.

123. As war is an extension of politics, advertising is an extension of merchandising. No advertising campaign is worth its salt unless it reflects a sound merchandising strategy, policy, and concept.

124. The fashion customer is always interested in something new. Designer names were and are news and exciting for this customer.

125. Retailers should not only have promoted the new designers; they should have financially invested in the designers so they could monitor their distribution and also benefit from their licensing revenues.

126. Sometimes a change in ownership can be a negative to a career, as was my experience when G. Fox was acquired by May Department Stores. Other times it can be positive, such as Bergdorf Goodman to General Cinema. So, remember the ball bouncing in the pinball machine. It can bounce good and sometimes bad.

127. When there is little control over the situation, a lot of luck helps.

128. When the business isn't doing well and has weak management, consultants are helpful, but there is never a substitute for professional management, professional management being defined as "proven professionals."

129. When searching for a key executive in an organization, it is critical to define clearly to all those making the decision that they agree on what the highest standards and objectives are for that position. In addition, every resource available must be employed, from personal contacts to a professional executive recruiter familiar with all aspects of that industry's inner workings. Unimpeachable references are also an imperative requirement.

130. Never be satisfied with your progress. There is always another idea, different from your competition. Competition must always be looked at as a threat to your business success. It should be studied carefully, and fought aggressively.

131. Being a good businessperson also means being a good citizen. As high standards are required in a successful business, so they are required in the society that surrounds us. Catering to the lowest common denominator will eventually bring you there.

132. The saying "When in Rome, do as the Romans do" applies to all countries and unusual environments.

133. Whenever in a situation different from what you are used to, let yourself be advised by an experienced person.

134. In the retail fashion business it is imperative to have a knowledgeable fashion director, as well as an imaginative publicity director, as it is to have "a nose" in the perfume business. Both perform a function that is unique and special that will lead to success.

135. Whenever an opportunity presents itself, even though it may not be in the short- or long-range plan, examine the opportunity very carefully from every angle. Use all your best thinking, as well as the counsel of those who work with you. President Kennedy said, "I use all the brains I have and all that I can borrow before making an important decision."

136. The principal of any retail store who wants his or her establishment to be a dominant fashion force must realize that a professional fashion director is as important as any newspaper editor, financial director, or operating officer.

137. Opportunity is always there if you continue to look for it. The phrase "It is not what you know, but who you know" is only half correct. I believe "It is what you know and who you know" that brings success to your dreams and ambitions.

138. No matter what business, basic principles that successful executives have proven sound will, more times than not, lead to success.

INDEX

Page numbers in italics refer to images.

casual Fridays, 237
catalog retailing, 249
CFDA (Council of Fashion
    Designers of America),
    71
Chanel, 61, *126*
Chaney, William, 215
charity events, 57–66, *117*
Charles A. Stevens & Co.,
    212
Charvet, 41, 165–66
Christian, John, 26, *27*
Circuit City, 189
Claiborne, Liz, 152–53
closeout stores, 227–28
Columbia, 6–7
cosmetics, 184
    see also Estée Lauder
Courrèges, André, *112*
Cuneo, Peter, 191
customers, 10, 33, 187–90,
    213, 224–26, 228
    focus groups, 8, 10
    "lessons learned," 33, 40,
        209, 213, 226, 228,
        242, 251
    loyalty, 205–9
    luxury-brand customers,
        229–31
    men, 232–35
    What is a customer?,
        189–90

customer service, 187–90,
    224–26
    and the Internet, 251
    telephone manners, 240–42

Dalí, Salvador, 232
de la Renta, Oscar, *141*,
    154–55
Delman, 114–15, 173
designer exclusivity, 46–47,
    219
Princess Diana, 85–88, 94
direct mail, 10, 197, 249–50
display windows, 197
Dorsey, Hebe, 94
dressing, 236–39
Duke, Doris, *63*
Dumas, Jean-Louis, 114–15

Eberstadt, Freddie, *63*
Elkin, Steve, 104–105
Erasmus Hall, 2, 6
Estée Lauder, *58*, 100, 103,
    159–60, *161*, 162
Esterhazy, Louise, 71
Evans, Charles, *22*, 23
exclusivity, 46–47, 219

de la Falaise, Maxime, *30*
fashion events, 71–75, *76–81*
    see also charity events;
        fashion shows